"Managers are a dime a dozen, but leaders are priceless. Teaching principles as solid as setting expectations, and as radical as understanding love, Gerry Czarnecki's 10 Principles in *Lead with Love*, put the leader's focus where it belongs--on finding, developing, and rewarding teams of outstanding performers. Any manager aspiring to superior leadership would be wise to study Gerry's advice."

H. Wayne Huizenga, Chairman, Huizenga Holdings

"In *Lead with Love*, Gerry Czarnecki shows us how to achieve our human potential and elevate our lives, and the lives of those around us. His 10 Principles support his vision of helping all associate to achieve their dreams. Gerry eloquently argues that individuals and organizations achieve peak performance only when the leaders reach inside their souls to lead with the first principle of Love. He will Wow your souls."

Mark Victor Hansen, Co-Creator of Chicken Soup for the Soul, and America's Ambassador of Possibility

"*Lead with Love* is unlike any book on leadership and management I have ever read. It is extremely practical. A remarkable book."

Donald Humphreys, Senior Vice President and Treasurer, Exxon/Mobil Corporation

"A gutsy book. Gerry Czarnecki has spoken honestly about responsibilities and motivations at work in a way that no one has done before. *Lead with Love* should be read by anyone interested in management and organization."

Professor Howard Thomas, Dean, Warwick Business School

"*Lead with Love* is an engaging and thought-provoking book. A cogent treatment of a very important topic."

David Heenan, Author, Flight Capital and Double Lives

"Lead with Love is a unique book from a remarkable individual. Gerry Czarnecki's insights are priceless if you want to achieve peak performance in business and in life. *Lead with Love* will help all who read it understand the power of people-centric leadership in achieving extraordinary results. I highly recommend this book."

Ralph de la Vega, President and CEO AT&T Mobility And Consumer Markets

"Leaders often forget that it's all about putting people first. Lead with Love starts the exploration with that message, and ends by demonstrating the importance of passion in effective leadership. Gerry provides a roadmap for living it.

Graham Spanier, President, Pennsylvania State University

"In today's age of "management science," leadership too often takes a back seat to organizational metrics, systems and structures. However, Gerry Czarnecki's powerful new book, Lead with Love, strongly reminds us the leadership imbued with love of one's colleagues is the real difference maker in building high performing organizations. If you are a CEO, an aspiring leader or a manager of people in any part of an organization and haven't already read Czarnecki's work, this is a terrific place to start!"

Sean C. Rush, President & CEO, JA Worldwide

"Deadly accurate. Don't try leading an organization of any size without reading this book."

Merrill (Tony) McPeak. General Merrill A. McPeak
(Ret.)Chief of Staff, US Air Force, 1990-94

"A MUST read for today's leaders, Gerry Czarnecki starts the book with the concept of Love and ends the book talking about Passion. These two words act as bookends for the power of the full 10 leadership principles contained in the book. No organization should lead without it!"

Bill Reicherter, Founder & CEO B R Signs, Inc. & IS Franchising 4 You?

"The timely and inspiring message of Lead with Love is not just that we can lift ourselves, but is all about what we can, indeed must, do to lift people who work to do their part to help organizations achieve peak performance."

Mike Davidson, Chief Agency and Marketing Officer,
State Farm Insurance Companies.

"I found the ideas and strategies in Gerry Czarnecki's Lead with Love to be just as useful in my volunteer work as the board chair of a non-profit charity as it was in my professional work as a corporate executive. Everyone can find someplace in their lives where these concepts will help them improve themselves and the organizations they work in and care about."

Jeanne Connelly, Connelly Consulting LLC

"I couldn't put Gerry Czarnecki's new book _Lead with Love_ down on I started turn its pages. From the first to the last page its filled with insights and principals designed to improve its readers leadership and management skills -- and yes the bottom line results. Gerry shows clearly one can maintain your integrity and principals and still thrive in this very competitive global economy. This book should be required reading of every University MBA program in the country."

James DiGeorgia, Editor and Publisher, Gold and Energy Advisor

"Finally, in _Lead With Love_, we have a book on leadership that is practical and down-to-earth and is based on common sense. It is a "how-to" explanation that is applicable to leaders of all kinds at all levels. I wish I had read this 40 years ago."

Jay Stone, Vice President, Van Scoyoc Associates, Inc.

"In his own down to earth style, in _Lead with Love_, Gerry Czarnecki walks us through the concept of, 'What's love got to do with it?' He draws important distinctions like, comfort doesn't equal love and loving leaders still need direction and focus to succeed. With actionable scenarios and thought provoking leadership tips, this is an enjoyable guide to successful leadership."

Jacqueline Townsend Konstanturos, Founder
The Townsend Agency, CEO Restorative Remedies, LLC

"I have seen Gerry Czarnecki in action offering his wise insights and keen advice to top business executives. What an opportunity this book, _Lead with Love_, now offers readers to draw upon his inimitable guidance on being a leader."

James Kristie, Editor, Directors & Boards

"At a time when leadership is critical to the success of our way of life, Gerry Czarnecki has produced another of his books on what it takes to be a leader. This new book focuses on what leaders must do, not who they are. This book provides a solid, practical basis for executing leadership as well as management. If you have an organization, a vision, a mission, and a set of values and you stop one day and look behind you...and no one is there, then you need to read _Lead with Love_ as soon as possible. Don't let the word "love" scare you. It could save your organization."

Mike Greene, President, Video Dynamics Corporation

"Gerry Czarnecki's _Lead with Love_, is destined to generate a new genre of "How To" management books. Using language everyone understands and highlighting human emotions we all share, Mr. Czarnecki teaches competent Managers how to become effective Leaders. _Lead with Love_ should be mandatory reading in every MBA program curriculum."

Carlos A. Rodriguez, President & CEO,
Rodriguez & Co., Political/Public Affairs Consulting

"I served with Gerry on the board of an early stage company for three years. I witnessed him apply the concepts of Lead with Love and the impact it had on the success of this entity. The book provides a pathway to what it truly takes to be a great leader. He has emulated these truths and the impact was felt in many ways."

Richard Kohr, Jr., Chief Executive Officer, Evergreen Capital LLC

"Gerry Czarnecki has keen insight and a wealth of leadership experience that he brings to his latest book "_Lead with Love_." It's a worthwhile read for anyone in a leadership position, or aspiring to take on a leadership role."

Ed Galante, Senior Vice President (Retired), Exxon Mobil Corporation

"Gerry Czarnecki's concept of loving your associates is a powerful one for managers at any level of an organization from CEO to foreman. This book can be a useful guide for a successful career."

Walter Loewenstern, Co-founder ROLM Corporation.

"We often hear that an organization's most important asset is its employees – often referred to as the human factor. This book unlike any other helped me realize how to elevate my leadership skills by first leading with "love" while still driving for results. This is a must read for anyone who is looking to take their organization to the next level."

Rich Guidotti, Vice President & General Manager, AT&T

"Gerry Czarnecki's provocative message will challenge many of your most frequently held beliefs. This book provides candid, practical insight and advice on managing for results at firms of any size from an experienced leader."

Charles J Thayer, Chairman, Chartwell Capital Ltd

"When we inspire goodness, truth, and beauty we accomplish greatness. <u>Lead with Love</u> shows how these noble values, shaped by a commitment to Love, convert ordinary existences into lives of unforgettable meaning and worth."

David Mathison: Publisher, BE THE MEDIA

"Gerry is an experienced and effective leader, who provides his skill and expertise through his insightful and thought provoking book, <u>Lead with Love</u>. This book is a must read for anyone who desires to successfully lead others."

Charles Brummell, Managing Director, Fox Court Associates, LLC

"Just when you think that no one can possibly write anything new and enlightening on management philosophy, Gerry Czarnecki has wonderfully pieced together his personal experiences and some generally accepted (but rarely consistently practices) principles into a powerful, thought-provoking set of principles on leadership of *any* group. The focal point, leading with love, should cause every manager to fundamentally re-think his/her approach to not only leading his/her own group, but interacting with anyone else in their organization … and beyond those bounds as well.'

Fred Portner, Chief Financial Officer, Best Tech Brands LLC

LEAD with LOVE

10 PRINCIPLES
*every leader needs to maximize potential
and achieve peak performance*

GERRY CZARNECKI

THE LEADERSHIP CZAR

MILTON RAE
PRESS

Lead With Love
10 Principles Every Leader Needs to
Maximize Potential and Achieve Peak Performance

Softcover ISBN: 978-0-98207-502-9

Hardcover ISBN: 978-0-98207-501-2

Library of Congress Control Number: 2009927107

Cover Design by Rachel Lopez • www.r2cdesign.com

In an effort to support local communities, raise awareness and funds, Morgan James Publishing donates one percent of all book sales for the life of each book to Habitat for Humanity. Get involved today, visit **www.HelpHabitatForHumanity.org**.

Dedication

To every leader who has struggled
to understand and exercise effective leadership,
only to find that organizations succeed
because of associates who achieve their dreams.

Acknowledgments

This book is the result of evolution and learning. My first book, *You're In Charge…What Now?*, is the foundation upon which this book is built. That book was dedicated to the first-level leader who actually "does the work" and leads … what I called the "work leader." From the responses I have received since its publication, there is no doubt in my mind that many work leaders gained from the principles outlined there. On the other hand, three things have happened since that book was published, and those three things have actually caused me to write this book.

First, I have experienced hundreds of seminars, taught classes, given speeches, and won consulting engagements based on the principles in that book, and my thinking has evolved, largely through those experiences. That evolution has caused me to change and expand the mnemonic from LEADER to LEADERSHIP. Nothing I focused on before is lost, but I have added some core principles that I believe round out the core actions of a great leader.

Second, many of those who read the book were not "work leaders," yet they told me that no matter what level they had attained, these principles applied to them. Ironically, I never doubted that they did, but I was amazed at how many "executives" were willing to admit that they too often had forgotten the importance of these behaviors as they moved up the organizational ranks and that they failed to apply these principles as they became more strategic and high level in their roles. In short, they said they found that the book helped them to be better leaders, even as CEOs. That finding was stunning, rewarding, and energizing.

Third, and perhaps most important, I have been amazed with the reaction by most readers to the first chapter in the first book. Most business book writers should know, certainly I did, that what they are saying is not likely to be breakthrough "new knowledge." A few authors have truly broken new ground—Peter Drucker, Tom Peters, Jerry Porras, and Jim Collins—but most of us hope to just communicate the core principles in a little bit better, or at least different, way. Certainly I have no illusions of anything of the order of magnitude of those mentioned, but I am now convinced that my focus on "love" was not just inflammatory but actually important new thinking. Almost every reader of that book came away from the experience identifying that concept as unusual and challenging. Not all agreed, but all were challenged to think about it as a behavioral driver.

In my first book, I gave recognition to Gail Melick, my first mentor, and acknowledged that he shaped much of my thinking on this matter. This book is the result of all those I have encountered since my first book. Because of you, I have grown in my thinking, and perhaps most important, concluded that I must stress the convictions I have about the importance of love in the leadership role. That conviction led to the name of the book and has led to my making certain that that theme pervades every chapter.

This book is also the result of thousands of hours of working with leaders of organizations of a wide range of size, complexity, and type. I have worked with the leaders of Fortune 50 companies, privately held companies, closely held public companies, large and small not-for-profits, and even the boards of companies at which I was the principal shareholder. In addition, I have served many organizations in many leadership capacities, and my colleagues in those organizations continue to help me develop in my understanding of leadership. Each of these experiences has enriched my understanding, and I have grown immeasurably by those interactions. I owe each of them a huge debt of gratitude for helping me to better comprehend how leaders can apply leadership principles to change the course of their organizations.

Gerald M. Czarnecki
Boca Raton, Florida

Contents

INTRODUCTION
It's as Simple as the Word
L-E-A-D-E-R-S-H-I-P

This book is designed to help leaders use leadership as a competitive advantage. Sound principles of leadership can change the course of an organization at every level. Great leaders, with a keen sense of their role in leading the organization as a whole, can make a huge difference in the enterprise's ability to achieve superior, peak performance.

The original book in which I incorporated the core principles of the mnemonic LEADERS—*You're In Charge... What Now?*—was designed to help the first level of leaders achieve superior performance. Those principles have indeed helped thousands of leaders achieve greater success and superior results. That book focused on an organizational leader I called the "work leader." The "work leader" was defined as that leader who must mix being an individual performer and a leader at the same time.

This book is a logical extension of the principles outlined in my first book, but it does not focus on the "work leader" alone. Here, I hope that every leader at every level, from board member to first-level supervisor, will take the key leadership principles and apply them to their roles. These principles apply to every leader, no matter what the situation, from the coach of a Little League team to the CEO of a publicly traded company to the non-executive chairman of the board of a Fortune 50 company.

Every leader, each day, is charged with leading people whose work produces results. The direct and unambiguous impact leaders have on their associates is almost incalculable. Leaders make a huge difference

1

in any organization, and consequently it is essential that organizations provide all the support and counsel they can muster to help leaders excel.

There are leaders at various levels throughout the workplace. They range from the highest ranks in an organization to the lowest. More often than not, when professionals discuss the role of leadership in an organization, they focus on the very top of the traditional management pyramid. CEOs and other executives are typically the focus—and they should be. They set the "tone at the top" and that is critical to the overall success of the enterprise.

There are, however, many other layers in an organization at which leadership is just as important, perhaps even more so. Consider the importance of team members with a leadership mindset who:

- ➤ lead a team of colleagues on a strategy consulting engagement for a Fortune 500 company;
- ➤ lead a financial organization as the CFO of a Fortune 500 company;
- ➤ run a section of clerks who are responsible for processing accounts receivable payments;
- ➤ lead a team of doctors treating patients in an emergency room;
- ➤ manage a production line in the local automobile plant assembling 100 units a day;
- ➤ own and manage a lawn care service with its seven-member crew;
- ➤ manage an information technology project with its ten analysts;
- ➤ lead a manufacturing plant of 5,000 people as general manager;
- ➤ manage a retail store with nine sales clerks who need to sell a total of $250,000 each month if the store is to make money;
- ➤ head a product management team for a Fortune 100 company with a staff of five assistants;
- ➤ lead a sales team of three people that needs ten closes a week to make the month's sales goals;
- ➤ lead a team of engineers in a Fortune 50 company working on the development of a component for a new-generation aircraft;

> ➤ run a not-for-profit organization that has a budget of $1 million and employs five people who deliver services to the local community;
> ➤ own, manage, and style hair in a salon with $200,000 a year in revenue; or
> ➤ supervise a team of accountants who audit a number of public companies.

Each of these roles defines an activity that is often referred to as managing. All managers must be focused on results, and results are accomplished by the people in the organization who do the work. For this reason, the primary skill required to achieve peak performance results is the ability to energize the individuals—and the team—to achieve the unit's goals. That means these individuals must lead their associates who are doing the work.

For emphasis on this point, we can find no less a source than the insightful author, statesman, and intellectual John Gardner:

> Many writers on leadership take considerable pains to distinguish between leaders and managers. In the process leaders generally end up looking like a cross between Napoleon and the Pied Piper, and managers like unimaginative clods. This troubles me. I once heard it said of a man, "He's an utterly first-class manager but there isn't a trace of the leader in him." I am still looking for that man, and I am beginning to believe that he does not exist. Every time I encounter utterly first-class managers they turn out to have quite a lot of the leader in them.[1]

In my opinion, Gardner actually understates the point. It is impossible for a successful manager, in the long run, to be a bad leader. People will not continue to achieve for a failed leader. So, again, the practice of leadership is as important at the first level of management as it is at the highest—maybe even more so. These leaders get the work done, day in and day out.

This book focuses on what leaders do, not who they are. Much of the literature about managing focuses on the observations that great leaders are charismatic, trustworthy, honest, great examples, and so on. However, these abstract terms have a weak link to the reality of the world of work. Here, our focus is entirely on helping leaders do what will make them and their organizations successful. That means although leaders focus on the process of management, most also do some of the task work. In other words, leaders manage process, but they are probably also part of the process. It is impossible for most leaders to avoid "doing tasks"; however, the higher up the organizational pyramid organizational/management leaders climb, the less they are engaged in the actual hands-on tasks of day-to-day production.

A leading author on leadership, John Kotter, points out that "what a manager/leader does on a minute-minute, hour-hour basis rarely jibes with any stereotype with a manager, a heroic leader, or an executive, a fact that can create considerable confusion for those new to managerial jobs."[2] It is true that most leadership jobs are a blend of doing and leading, no matter what the level. Top-level leaders are involved in task work and must also spend substantial time reviewing reports and documents that are developed in order to brief them on the state of the organization. In some ways, these activities can cause leaders to see themselves more as "doers" and less as leaders. In the forthcoming chapters, I make the argument that leaders must resist the temptation to see themselves as "paper pushers" and concentrate more on their role as the ones who set the tone for the entire enterprise.

Becoming an Effective Leader

If you were recently thrust into a leadership position, you may feel unprepared for what is about to become the daily task of leading. Up to now, you were responsible for peak performance in your job. You may have been helping your fellow associates with their work, but your primary assigned tasks were individual ones. Your success was *your* success, your failure also *yours*. Most people who have taken on the leader role would admit that those were much simpler times. Yet almost everybody offered a promotion to leadership will grab it.

Most leaders start as people who do the work. They are assigned a set of duties that require them to create output in some work process. They might be accountants, teachers, salespeople, lawyers, engineers, research scientists, or even the legendary "mail room clerk." At some point, they get so good at the work they perform that somebody decides to put them in charge of other people doing the same tasks. Suddenly they are the leader. Sometimes overnight, they are assigned a leadership function and expected to do a new kind of job—to lead others instead of doing what they know how to do, which is to perform tasks. They become what I call "accidental leaders."

To some extent, these "accidental leaders" take these positions because they like the idea of being in charge. They may have been convinced that the former leader did not measure up and that they could do a better job. In other cases, they take these positions because they view the leader or manager tracks as the only way to achieve the fuller success they are seeking.

Whatever the case, if you are now a leader, you were assigned to the position because somebody decided that you could do it. Once you are on that track, you are going to be held accountable for peak performance results, and that will drive you to find ways to deploy the skills required. Most management training programs focus on the mechanics of managing projects or processes. The mechanics of management are important, but all too many failed managers have had those skills fine-tuned by traditional learning while learning little about how to lead people. Joe Batten said it well:

> Managers abound but leaders are still at a premium.
> Managers manage inventories, supplies, and data. They

are number crunchers. Leaders catalyze, stretch, and enhance people. They provide transcendent goals, creating a motivational climate.

Managers *push* and direct. Leaders pull and expect. Leaders are exhilarated by identifying and enhancing their people's strengths.

Despite the many books on management published in recent years, the MBA factories continue to turn out graduates woefully deficient in leadership insights, skills, and hands-on tools. Taking refuge behind reams of data is still appallingly common, but it is no substitute for true leadership.[3]

The decision-maker who put you "in charge" hopefully believes that you possess the knowledge, skills, and attitude necessary to succeed in that role. Now it is your job to assume the identity of "leader" and understand that your success will be your associates' success, and their failure will be your failure. The purpose of this book is to ensure that your leadership endeavors are successful.

On the other hand, some of you have been in charge of organizations for a long time. You have moved up the ranks and through successive promotions and are now at a level where you actually "do little real task work." Those of you in that position may have even more to gain from this book, because you have probably been drawn into doing so many things that have nothing to do with leading the people who work for you that you may have badly neglected the role of being the leader. Some of those things can be: relationships with customers, interface with the board of directors, participation in industry leadership roles, pro bono activities, strategic planning, etc. You could be so good at those other things that you spend virtually no time with those who report to you.

If that sounds familiar, then welcome to the role of senior executive. It is very easy for the senior executive to get so busy with "upward" and "sideward" relationships that he or she can forget completely about "downward." Every CEO knows this problem, but few actually do anything about it. One of the truly respected CEOs of the last thirty years, Jack Welch, made a habit of never letting himself forget this responsibility. Far too few in that CEO seat remember that the way an organization achieves is by the tone at the top finding its way down the organizational pyramid.

Defining Leadership

The definition of leadership has been explored by many authors, but I like the simple yet elegant definition John Gardner offers: "Leadership is the process of persuasion or example by which an individual (or leadership team) induces a group to pursue objectives held by the leader or shared by the leader and his or her followers."[4]

Contrary to the conventional wisdom that leadership is the province of presidents of countries and CEOs, this definition gives us freedom to use the concept far more broadly. It is this view of leadership that will guide us throughout our pursuit of defining what leaders do to create peak performance for all types of organizations. You can, as an individual and as a manager, be a leader. Indeed, every aspect of the job you have is one of leadership, and hence all the elements of leadership apply to you.

Leading from a Distance Is Different from Leading the Daily Execution

Most of us are fascinated with great leaders and the stories of their triumphs. However, the problem with using corporate, national, or sports leaders as our role models is that the world they operate in has no clear relationship to what most boards of directors must do. Books that define the characteristics of a great leader only help to confuse us when we try to apply them to the grind of our daily jobs. Learning how a mayor makes a strategic decision on when to deploy a police force in a crisis, how a governor decides to reduce the size of a $20 billion budget, or how a CEO acts to increase the profits of a $30 billion company has little meaning to an average leader who is concerned about running a branch office with a budget of less than $1 million. Knowing that Vince Lombardi shouted at each of his football players when they did something stupid on the playing field or that he created a new defensive alignment that gave him a competitive advantage in the National Football League has very little meaning to the director of a not-for-profit who needs to increase fund-raising in order to avoid a deficit for the year. Learning how the president of the United States leverages the knowledge of his cabinet to decide how to deal with a crisis in a third world country offers very little help to a corporate board of directors that just discovered the CEO is leaving and the organization has no clear successor in place.

Many of these well-known leaders of large organizations succeed because they have the unique ability to hire great people and then get out of the way. This concept is often touted as the key to a leader's success, and indeed for many at the top of very large organizations it is a critical skill. For most real-world leaders, however, that advice could be disastrous.

An organization's results depend on strategy and execution. Organizations must do the right tasks, but they must also do them the right way. Strategy sets the course for doing the right tasks; execution gets them done. Collins and Porras in their outstanding book *Built to Last* made the same point: "People don't work day-to-day in the big picture. They work in the nitty-gritty details of their company and its business. Not that the big picture is irrelevant, but it's the little things that make a big impression, that send powerful signals."[5] The top executives set the course; the lower level leader executes.

Boards of directors are simply too far away from the personnel who execute to have any real understanding of the probability of success. Boards must be able to evaluate the execution in the organization; they cannot simply "get out of the way." All too many boards have gotten out of the way, only to discover the corporation was not executing and, years later, that the corporation was failing.

A leader is a person who needs to get work done through a team of associates. This activity is what some would call managing. Managers have two tasks: (1) administration and (2) leadership. You could think of administration as all of those tasks that must be done in order to find the time to lead, such as filling out employment forms for new employees, turning in timecards for payroll, filling out budgets for accounting, ordering supplies, preparing reports to other managers, communicating with customers, checking production reports, paying taxes, reading reports from managers, talking to customers, and so on. Leadership generally means helping the people who work for you achieve the objectives of your organization. It is about getting the work done through people.

To be effective, each leader needs guidance as to what must be done each minute of each day. This book is designed to give you that guidance and help you become a better leader. What every leader yearns for are a few simple thoughts about how to make an organization successful. The principles in this book apply equally to the chair of the board of the local Red Cross affiliate, the head of the PTA, the supervisor of a team of accountants, the owner of a small family company, the vice president of sales for a $25 million organization, the manager of a local bank branch, the CEO of a Fortune 500 multinational company, and anybody else who fills the role of leader. All of these people have one job in common: they are "in charge" in their capacity as leader. They generally have a boss with expectations that they and their team will perform well and accomplish the organization's goals.

Getting the organization to achieve is essential, and a great leader can make a huge difference in the whole organization's success. John Kotter gets it right in his book *The Leadership Factor* when he says:

> Leadership, with an "l," is of incredible importance
> in today's world. Its cumulative effect often makes the

difference between dreadfully stifling and unresponsive bureaucracies and lively, adaptive organizations. At the level of a single individual, it sometimes occurs in such a subtle way that we don't even notice it. That is especially true if the vision is borrowed (developed not by the individual but by someone else) and the number of people who must be led is very small, as is so often the case. Needless to say, it would help greatly if we could get more people to think of leadership in the small "l" sense and not just in the larger-than-life "L" sense.[6]

Making the Job Simple but Not Easy

Although leaders do many tasks, you can boil down the role of a leader into ten key principles. Each principle is a simple concept to explain but not always easy to accomplish. To make being a leader as simple as possible, then, the goal is to get rid of everything that does not apply to small unit leadership and focus on key elements that will make every leader great.

Our journey will take us through the mnemonic LEADERSHIP … each letter represents the essence of a key principle for peak performance. The leadership principles start with L for love, followed by E for expectations, A for assignment, D for development, E for evaluate, R for rewards, S for systems, H for humor, I for integrity, and P for passion. The words are important keys to remembering the concepts, which were introduced and presented in my first book, *You're In Charge…What Now?*. In this book, these concepts will be applied to individuals and their leadership challenges at every level. These concepts have one message: focus on the principles, and complex and confusing issues can be ignored.

In the world of work, leading is useless if it does not result in the achievement of organizational goals. If a board leader does not help the organization achieve its goals, then board leadership has failed. Leading successful organizations is hard work. It is not based on charisma, although that quality can help. It is not based on intellect, although being smart is always advantageous. If you want to be a great board member, you need to practice these ten key activities every time you work on the organization's activities. When you are at board meetings, there can be no days off. Leadership is a real job, and it requires a complete commitment to these actions—not just believing in them, but doing them every time you are engaged as a board member.

The great news is, if you execute these ten key principles, you will have a very high probability of success. The bad news is, if you lose your resolve to follow the LEADERSHIP principles, you will most likely fail. There is little room for error. This set of actions is so refined that if one principle is violated, you will substantially increase your chance for failure. Each principle relies on the others. These may be simple concepts, but focused, hard work is required.

The Law of Administrivia—The Greatest Barrier to Leadership Success

In my first book, I talked about the concept of the Law of Administrivia, and I have had innumerable people tell me that this concept not only resonated with them but was almost the "bane of their existence." I will admit, I fight daily to avoid falling into the trap of following the path to administrivia and wasting my day. You too must avoid this trap. I have repeated this section here, just in case you missed it in my first book.

One of the long-standing principles in economics is called Gresham's law. It states that if two currencies are circulating in an economy—one a high-quality currency that everybody trusts and believes in and the other a poor-quality currency that everybody thinks has substantial risk—then the bad currency will drive out the good currency. This means everybody will want to hoard the "good" currency and give the "bad" to other people whenever they can.

In leading, the same principle applies. Call it the "Law of Administrivia": *required or less useful activity drives out desirable and useful activity.* In other words, people will do the tasks they think are easy, trivial, and required first, in order to get them out of the way. Then, with the time left over, they will do what is desirable or useful but not required. In short, people will do trivial administrative tasks (administrivia) first just to avoid trouble with the boss. Then they concentrate on that which they know to be useful. Unfortunately, this creates a dilemma since the amount of administrivia grows once the boss concludes you are able to handle what you have already been given to accomplish. Eventually you do less and less of what you want or need to do and much more of the administrative work. Worse still, since administrivia is usually easy work, while being a leader is hard work, guess which work you end up spending more time on? There is almost no other answer than ... the easy job. After a while, that is all that gets done. So we focus on the required, the trivial, and maybe even the useless, while the truly meaningful is driven out.

Of course, not all administrative work is meaningless or trivial. Indeed, much of the success in an organization rests on process and process controls. However, if administrative tasks are the only activities a leader has time for, then these tasks will ultimately hamper the leader's effectiveness. Frequently, we forget how much time and energy leadership really takes. If leaders use planning, organizing, and control as effective tools to handle the workflow, then much more time can be reserved for leader work. If the administrivia does not free you but rather consumes your day, then leadership will be driven out. If the administrative work is effective, then you will be free to lead.

Parts of the Law of Administrivia have been recognized for some time. In 1968, Saul Gellerman wrote, "The simple fact is that most managerial jobs are already more than full-time jobs. The typical manager has more than enough to worry about. His typical solution is to arrange his problems in order of priority, deal with the ones he has time for, and just ignore the rest. In other words, that which is urgent gets done and that which is merely important frequently doesn't."[7]

12

What I am adding is this: frequently the urgent is not essential to the mission but rather just easier to ask for or to accomplish.

Look at the activities you engage in and determine if they are critical to your efforts to succeed. If you are spending time doing tasks other than the ten LEADERSHIP actions, then you are wasting time. If your efforts to lead are frustrated because you are preoccupied with administrative tasks, then you need to find a way to break loose from the constraints of those activities. You will find leader actions need not be so time-consuming that you have no time for anything else. In fact, if you do the leader work well, you will have plenty of time for administrative tasks. The only way you are going to break loose is to realize leader work is the only way to achieve your goals and objectives. It is the "good work." That is one of the goals of this book—to help you become a believer in the ten principles of great leadership and act accordingly by fighting the tendency to be ruled by the Law of Administrivia.

Getting Maximum Benefit—What's Ahead?

This book is designed as a leader's handbook for success. It is structured so you cannot merely read the information; it also asks you to think about it and apply it to your life and work. Each chapter follows the mnemonic, with key points often built into the subheadings. Throughout every chapter, you will also find "Leadership Tips" that offer you practical advice on what to do to achieve peak performance results. These tips outline some tasks that will get you moving along the path to effective, practical application of the ten principles, but they will not guarantee success. Remember, leading is simple work that is tough to do.

At the end of each chapter, you will find a case study that poses a real-life situation that could happen—and actually did. These studies are summaries of actual situations. The names and businesses are modified for privacy reasons. You are encouraged to read the case, preferably with a small group of peers, and use it as a vehicle for discussion of the situations and challenges depicted. Try some role-playing to determine how you might have handled the situation differently. This is a strategic way to practice executing the LEADERSHIP principles in each chapter.

In addition, a reading list is included in each chapter for you to review and experiment with. No reader will read every book, but these references offer you solid sources of more in-depth thinking on the topics in each chapter. Some sources are referred to in the text, others are references for key ideas, and others are simply good supplements to the concepts in each chapter. As you will discover later, the continuous learning process is vital to your leadership development. Keep this book at hand and refer back to it when you think you need better understanding, or even a little reminder.

Leaders Make a Difference; Be a Great One

Even the most strategic thinkers understand the role leaders play. In his book *Pana Management*, Morimasa Ogawa writes, "There are two types of management today. One is management for the future. Also known as strategic management. The other type of management is management for the present, the hands-on approach that ensures the survival of an enterprise here and now. Management for the present is what all employees are doing every day in every department."[8]

As a leader, you must make certain that your leadership is focused on "the present." You must lead your associates if you want to assure the enterprise's survival. Become a leader who practices the ten key principles of LEADERSHIP. They are hard work for even the best leader, but when practiced every day, they will become second nature to you. Stay on track with these simple yet not easy principles, and peak performance can be yours.

Each chapter in this book describes a key leadership principle for you to apply to help others. At the end of each chapter, there is a section dedicated to helping you as a leader; apply these principles as you "lead yourself." Every leader is a human being—an individual first, a leader second. Focusing on yourself is not selfish; it is necessary to care for your "self" in order to give of that self to others. Loving leaders use expectations, assignment, development, evaluation, rewards, systems, humor, integrity, and passion to assure their associates' success. It follows that you must apply these principles to yourself. If peak performance and success are your goals, make leading yourself a priority equal to that of leading your associates. In the same way you make certain your associates fulfill their potential, so must you make certain you fulfill your potential. Be open to opportunities for improvement, work to develop yourself through effective evaluations of your performance, and have an improvement plan that structures your efforts for personal development. The key is to recognize that the steps to improvement are all interrelated and not always sequential. Dave Heenan, in his book *Double Lives*, suggests:

> Cultivate the art of making yourself up as you go along. The process of rediscovery will expand your world. As Jean-Jacques Rousseau once put it, "The world of reality has its limits; the world of imagination is boundless."
>
> Don't draw lines that limit what you are or are not. Doing so may eliminate novel invitations and the chance of switching gears. Don't edit out choices or become pigeonholed. Do be on a continuous hunt for what you love, what you do well, and what just piques your curiosity.[9]

CHAPTER ONE

LOVE—Friends Like but Leaders Love

Stop. Do not write off this concept. Everything a leader does begins with a capacity and commitment to love. This is the theme and central core of this book, and there is little doubt the use of that word will rankle the typical leader. But you got past the title of the book, so now you are about to find out how this book uses that term, and why it is the key word in the book.

You must understand that I am not a product of the "flower child culture." I am an early baby boomer who never even came close to being part of the drug- using, peace movement. I was not a protester against the war in Vietnam, and indeed, I was on active duty as a US Army captain during the Vietnam War. I went back to graduate school when the war was unpopular, and I attended classes with the students who turned the country's attention from Vietnam, but a "peacenik" I was not.

If you look at any recount of my leadership and managerial history (www.geraldmczarnecki.com), you will find that I do not even have a "soft" reputation. Throughout most of my professional leadership career, I have been a change agent. Some will call that a euphemism for "tough guy who fires people." Indeed, in some ways, that was true. As a change agent, I spent much of my time fixing broken organizations. Many times, that meant terminating personnel. In short, I have legitimately been seen as a firefighter who did what it took to save organizations and jobs.

I make these points about myself because people who have worked closely with me over the years know that the principles in this chapter guide my every action. The principle of love drives my every leadership act, and I hope that you will read this chapter to understand why I believe that any leader, whose objective is to achieve peak performance and results consistently over the long run, must begin with love.

This chapter leads off the series of key principles reflected in the word LEADERSHIP, but this key idea about love ends up in the title for only one reason. Organizations, no matter how technical, no matter how mechanical, no matter how structured, are comprised of people working together to accomplish a mission or a goal. Take the people away and there is no organization; there are ideas, theories, even dreams, but without people there is nothing but infrastructure, not organization.

Since people make up the essence of organizations, people working together in some type of structure are the essence of how goals are achieved. Science, technology, processes, real estate, machines, natural resources—all are brought together by the humans who "band together" to accomplish a task, series of tasks, and ultimately a goal. The economists define the factors of production as land, labor, capital, and entrepreneurship. For our purposes, these factors are all combined into an organization that uses those factors to create results and, for the economist, goods and services that will have value in a market system.

Since people are why these resources are brought together, and since people are the glue and the brain of this organizational entity, we are driven to focus on how those people function, how they work together, and how their pooling of efforts creates value to the society. It is this pooling together, this set of human interactions, that makes it possible for organizations to achieve goals. This is not a philosophical treatise; it is a reality. Without people there would be no goals; without people there would be no achievement of the goals.

With that, the role of the leader becomes much clearer. The leader is the one who assembles the people and the various other "factors of production" to achieve the goals or, in our society, to create goods and services. Most economists who added the concept of entrepreneurship to the classic "factors of production" were forced to admit that there needed to be something that organized the factors of land, labor, and capital. We who have led organizations know that the term *leader* is much more reflective of the thing that ties the factors together.

Love is not used in this chapter to be inflammatory or sensational, although there are some who will charge that is my intent. *Love* is not just a word being used to carry a revolutionary message. It is the only word that can define the essence of this book. Once again, love is at the heart of all leadership activity, and it is that core concept that is embedded in every chapter of this book.

Love. In order to delve more deeply into this word, we actually need to look into some history, in particular, Greek and Hawaiian history. Let's start with the Greeks. What does the word *love* mean, especially for us in this context? The idea of love having a place in the workplace may be disorienting, especially if you're thinking of the kind of love the Greeks called "eros," what we know as sexual or erotic love. Obviously, eros is not the appropriate type of love for leaders to practice in the workplace. Indeed, inappropriate sexual relationships with a coworker—or worse, a subordinate—hold the potential for tragedy for all concerned.

The Greeks also used the word *philia*, which defined another type of love—the love that we have for family. When William Penn first settled in the New World, he named his first and most important city Philadelphia, "the city of brotherly love." The Greek word *philia* was at the heart of the name of his new city. He dreamed Philadelphia would be a city where people would treat each other as brothers.

The concept of brotherly love, or love of family, is a warm and sensitive type of love. It avoids the erotic or sexual aspects of eros, but goes well beyond friendship. The Greeks, and much of Western civilization, believe the bond between family members, in general, far exceeds that of any other relationship. Most of us would agree that our relationships with our family members are strong and critical elements of our own personal development.

This type of unconditional love has great emotional and spiritual appeal. Unfortunately, leaders cannot be this emotionally tied to those for whom leadership is their duty. In many ways, the unconditional nature of this type of love can be more damaging than helpful to a leader. Leaders of organizations, such as boards of directors, have a responsibility to be judgmental. Also, they must be focused on an organization's progress toward and achievement of goals and objectives.

Whether you are a non-executive chair of a religious college board, a development committee chair of a non-profit organization, a council member representing your constituents in a city government, or the chair of an audit committee for a huge public corporation, you have a duty to your group, and to your constituents, to achieve goals. As good as unconditional love may feel in any of those settings, any team member who is not pulling in the same direction is a potential risk to the objectives. You must be prepared to focus on achievement, in many cases to the detriment of an obstructing individual. Brotherly love probably will not help you take the actions necessary to persist on the course to goal alignment and achievement. Indeed, if your affection is so strong that it supersedes your duty to the mission of your organization, it may hinder your effectiveness.

So, let's move on to the third Greek word for love, *agape.* This word reflects the notion that we, as members of the human species, have a special duty to love other members of the species. This love for humankind is the form of love that drives activists to support elimination of the death penalty, causes philanthropists to give vast sums to charity, inspires caring people to volunteer in third world countries, and leads people to help those affected by disasters. We all have that altruistic part of us that wants to give to society or at least to others in need.

This is agape, the fine art—and even emotion—of loving people as members of humanity. It means we have a sensitivity to them that exceeds being polite. It means we pay attention to them, beyond just keeping them from being angry with us. It means helping them just because they are people—not necessarily because they are nice people—and helping them even when they find accepting help difficult. It means telling them bad news with sensitivity. It means not being brutally frank and blunt. In short, it means being aware of their needs, feelings, and difficulties. This type of caring is discussed in many ways by many authors. John Maxwell says it very explicitly: "Effective Leaders know that you must have to touch people's hearts before you ask them for a hand. That is the Law of Connection. All great communicators recognize this truth and act on it almost instinctively. You can't move people to action unless you first move them with emotion. The heart comes before the head."[10]

So, now what about the Hawaiians, and how can the residents of that far-off island chain be of any help? Hawaiians have a unique culture, formed by their great reliance on and attachment to the land. After the brutal consolidation of power by a warlord, King Kamehameha, the Hawaiian culture settled in for a long era of peace and relative prosperity. The culture created a sense of community and relied on a deep commitment to extended family. In addition, during that period, a culture that was highly isolated, yet homogeneous, became a culture of warmth and human sensitivity.

This cultural fact was evidenced in many aspects of the language, but no single word reflected that culture more than the word *aloha*. Most modern-day visitors to the islands think of the word *aloha* as a greeting having one of two meanings, hello or goodbye. Indeed, that is the most common use of the word, but it is actually the least meaningful. In the Hawaiian culture, *aloha* has many meanings and many uses, but the true importance of the word rests in its use to mean "love." When a Hawaiian says to you, "Aloha," what is really being said is "I extend my sense and emotion of love to you." If you are arriving, it means "welcome with love"; if you are departing, it means "go with love."

Indeed, those who have visited the islands may remember that the Hawaiian people express the culture as being a manifestation of the "Aloha Spirit." Therein lies the true meaning. *Aloha* means that "I will live in and among my society with my fellow citizens with a spirit of love." This is the true meaning of love for the Hawaiian culture. To live in love is to live at peace with oneself and with nature. It is this commitment to the love of humanity that defines the ancient Hawaiian culture, and it is this spirit of aloha that can define what is meant by love as the first principle of leadership.

I do not want to suggest that the Hawaiian culture is one without conflict and tension. Indeed, in recent years, there has been great tension in the society. But the root of the ancient Hawaiian traditions is "aloha," and the core values of the society demand a respect for humans and for nature. The small island state depends on a quality balance with nature and with the humanity assembled on their isolated islands. We in the rest of the world have much more opportunity to feel disconnected from each other and from nature, but the roots of our existence are embedded in each other and in nature as well.

It is this connection with humans and the desire, even need, to love and be loved as humans that define our uniqueness as a species. We may be the only species that feels this type of deep connection, and that factor makes us need to complete ourselves by beginning all our relationships with a connection that the Hawaiians called "aloha." It is this sense of aloha (love) that must precede our actions as leaders. When we feel that emotion, only then can we take actions that reflect a true concern for the humans over whom we maintain oversight, governance, and dominion. These functions are reliant on our ability to be servants to their needs while at the same time committing our energy to achieve the goals of the organization.

Why Not Like Instead of Love?

You may ask, "Why use the word *love* when the word *like* would be easier? Why not say that every leader must like people?"

For our purpose, the word *love* is more accurate and less confusing than the word *like*. Indeed, the proposition that leaders must like those they lead is flawed. When you like a person, what does that mean? Usually it means that person's personality characteristics, core beliefs, character traits, or even physical appearance, for some reason, appeal to either your emotions or logical thought. The person may have treated you nicely, smiled at you on a day you were unhappy, complimented you when you needed confidence building, or helped you think through a personal or business problem. You may even have an unexplained bond with that person, which made you feel an emotional attraction almost immediately. You may have nothing in common or everything in common, but you feel comfortable being around that person.

In the same way, liking your associates can help you to enjoy the people you lead. It makes you feel good to lead people you like. In turn, since the chemistry usually goes both ways, the people you are leading will probably like you and feel good about you. If all of this good comes out of liking, then what is wrong with the idea that you should like the people you lead?

Here's what's wrong: How many situations have you been in where you could say that you liked everybody in the group you were leading? If you have a group of two people, then you might expect that you will like both of them. However, most of us are charged with the responsibility of leading larger groups. If you are a sales manager who takes over a sales force of ten, the odds of not liking at least one person in that group are much greater.

Let's also hypothesize that the one person you do not like, for whatever reason, is also the top salesperson in the group and has the highest customer loyalty. In addition, that person has the best relationship with the manufacturing division and has always had the highest peer group ratings as well. At this point you might say, "If this person is that good, then obviously I would like her." Indeed, that might be true. The opposite happens frequently as well. You can have a top performer you truly dislike. If you have been a leader for any period of time, you have been in that situation and probably have struggled with the consequences.

If liking is a requirement of good leadership, how can you lead this person? By that definition, you cannot. So what do you do? Your dislike usually becomes a barrier to communication. If you do not like a person, it is very difficult to hide your dislike. The other person will sense how you feel and begin to react negatively to you as well. Slowly, you begin to distance yourselves from each other in an effort to avoid the undesirable contact. Worse still, you will invariably become overly critical of the person. Eventually these tensions will result in either termination or transfer of the subordinate. Bias wins every time.

Like and You May Be Sorry

Just as "philia," or brotherly love, can be damaging for leaders, so too can liking be dangerous. You may decide to be the leader of only those you like so you will not be challenged by conflict. That is often the next step along the destructive road of leading by liking. Since you want to like everybody who works for you, you begin the process by favoring the ones you like. In many cases, you look past the weaknesses of those you like and become highly critical of those you do not like. The process of favorites or "teacher's pets" begins. Even though your intentions may be honest and pure, you begin purging your staff of all those whom you do not like. Before you are finished, you have a team of people you like. It may or may not be a great team, but you like the team members and they like you. Maybe they are all friends as well. This friendship will probably influence your decisions, on occasion to the detriment of the organization. Bias wins again.

What is wrong with these scenarios? You could argue that nothing destroys a team more than a person who just does not fit in. Indeed, that can be very true. One rotten apple can spoil the basket. But what if the rotten apple is one of the people you like? Doesn't that make the problem more complex and sometimes painful? This is especially true if the friend has come to believe that the relationship with you is more important than the leadership relationship. Remember, as a leader your primary mission is to drive peak performance, not build a team of people you enjoy being with. That may make going to work fun, but it may also create serious conflict for you when a friend fails to achieve peak performance. Unfortunately, when this condition exists, leaders have a tendency to ignore the problem until the entire basket is rotten. Again, bias wins.

> A more common problem is a leader's inability to see weakness in a liked person. We all have a tendency to overlook, if not ignore, weaknesses in the people we like. Indeed, we have a tendency to inflate their strengths as well. As a result, we may be so completely blinded that we cannot truly be objective about performance. Remember, as leaders we are almost always accountable, either to ourselves or to a higher authority, for results that match the goals or objectives of the organization or unit. If we are blinded by liking, then we will never be able to evaluate the performance of the group or an individual in it. Often this situation causes shortfalls in performance or failure to achieve goals. At that point, most of us will attribute the failure to external factors rather than conclude that we have failed ourselves or that the team or its members have failed. Bias wins again.

Keep that notion of chemistry, or people liking each other, in mind. If a team is formed from a group of people who do not like each other, it is important that they learn to love each other. This sense of caring, in spite of the lack of liking, is crucial to team success. You do not need liking to create warmth; you need love. For this reason, when Allan Cox talks of warmth in *The Making of the Achiever*, we assume he means the kind of caring that comes from loving your associates. "Warmth is catching. It is easy to discern those companies where warmth in management has caught on. From first contact with the headquarters receptionist to the head of custodial services in an outlying plant, a visitor who walks the halls of a warm company and chats with its people senses the team-play and pride that pervade its atmosphere."[11]

AVOID THE LIKING TRAP

- You probably do not like at least one person who works for you today. Make three lists: (1) all the qualities you do not like about that person; (2) all the good qualities of that same person; (3) that person's primary duties and objectives. Now evaluate that person's performance against his or her objectives.
- Pick the one person you like best in your work unit and make the same three lists and do the same performance evaluation.
- Now compare the two sets of lists and evaluations. Answer this question: which person is the better performer, and why?
- There are probably several people who work for you that you like. Are any of them friends of yours? How long have they been friends? Do you socialize with them? How did you get to be the boss of the unit? Did you work in that unit alongside your friends, or did you come from outside the work unit? How do you feel about being your friends' boss? How do they feel about it? What would you change, if anything, about your unit and the staffing? What will you change in how you are managing the unit and the people you like?
- Have you ever fired a friend? Have you ever been fired by a friend? Are you still friends? What did you learn from the experience?

Back to Love

The contrast between "like" and "love" is both striking and critical. You can love (agape) people and not like them. No one is capable of liking everybody in the human species, but we can love (agape) everybody. As a leader, you must be able to care for all the members of your group, whether you like them or not. Only in that way can you give to your associates the commitment of truth, unbiased behavior, and help in achieving their goals.

Effective leaders have a strong ability to communicate their love to the group they are leading. Regardless of the dynamics of the day-to-day behavior of the leader, the group members must perceive they are being loved. Vince Lombardi was, as many great football coaches are, notorious for yelling insults at his players. Yet, in the face of such apparent disrespect, Lombardi was a loved coach who earned affection because players knew he loved them.

Leadership style is not the issue. Style is a description of perceived patterns of behavior, not necessarily a reflection of the internal capacity to love. In some style or personality types, it may take a little longer to determine if the capacity to love is present, but the lack of that capacity is almost always obvious. It seems that you can always detect a mean streak, or a lack of love, much faster than you can identify a real capacity to love.

Don't Fake It

It is almost impossible to hide a lack of love. Somehow those who pretend to have agape seem to give themselves away. "All the world is a stage," Shakespeare said, and many leaders are great actors. Some acting skill is probably helpful because even the most sincerely loving leader sometimes has a bad day. At these times, acting that provides encouragement and enthusiasm can often be a valuable leadership tool for the leader. On the other hand, people in leadership positions who continually pretend to be loving ultimately create trauma for those they lead. It is irrelevant how good the acting is; a leader's actions will speak louder than words or body language. Over time it is almost impossible for a "non-loving" person to hide the lack of human caring and agape.

The Pain of Working without a Loving Boss

Most of us have worked for non-lovers. One boss made me feel uncomfortable just being in his presence. I was his chief financial officer (CFO), and very early on he made it clear that he knew my job better than I did. He never actually had to say anything to cause me to doubt myself. After several months of this unexplained fear, I dreaded going to see him. And the situation was getting worse, not better. Each encounter created another bad experience for me, and probably for him as well.

I had a difficult time understanding what was happening to me until one day when we were discussing another person who had caused some difficulties in the company, and he said to me, "I do not trust him, but then, I do not trust anybody. And you, Gerry, your problem is you trust people. My advice to you is to recognize that the people who work for you are just human resources of the business, and you need to use them as if they are expendable. The only thing that matters is that we get the job done, and that means you need to check up on everything those people do." (As you might expect, I was working for a different company in less than six months.) This boss never understood that love and trust are the foundation of all human relationships. In fact, he never could check up on everybody all the time, and ultimately his subordinates failed him and the company. He never evolved into a leader, and he sank along with the company as it went into tragic decline. In this case, his employees' failure was his.

Agape is a state of the rational mind as much as it is an emotion. Loving others does not guarantee they will love you. Indeed, if you trust people and they do not reciprocate, you will have trouble. That is why some, like my infamous boss, would say you should never trust anyone. It is true that some people whom you love as humans will not repay your trust. Some people in this world are lazy, dishonest, uncaring, unloving, or just plain incompetent. However, no leader can be effective without a deep love for people as human beings.

The spirit of aloha is not always easy to follow. Many times in your career, you will encounter somebody who simply is not "likeable." That is the real test of aloha. It is not our responsibility to like our associates, but it is our responsibility to have aloha for them. When I lived in Hawaii, because so much of the culture was shaped by the "aloha spirit," it was impossible to not have aloha on my mind. Even those of us who were not native Hawaiians were always reminded of the aloha culture, and I know that it influenced how I reacted. Most of us in the workplace do not have that factor "keeping us honest," so we must rely on our commitment to be great leaders.

We leaders need to have love at the heart of everything we do because we are responsible for the success of our associates. At times, that love will be reflected in a sensitivity to an associate's anxiety; at other times, it will require high standards and expectations to focus an associate on achievement; at other times, it will mean reinforcing a successful action; and at other times, it will mean disciplining a serious misstep. All of these efforts will require more than just a mechanical effort. They require that extra measure of emotional sensitivity that is embodied in the concept of agape. *Only* when you love your associates can you perform these responsibilities with the sensitivity, compassion, and firmness required to assure successful goal achievement.

The Concept of Tough Love

The concept of "tough love" is very similar. It essentially means that parents need to love their children so much that they are able to be firm in their discipline process—to be tough, but with love. In the same way, as leaders we must care so much (love) that we are able to reinforce the required behavior through the tough discipline essential to the development of our staff. Love does not need to be soft to be real.

Remember, the objective here is the achievement of goals by your associates. Indeed, not just achievement but peak performance. That means you must lead them to success by helping them incorporate behaviors that will get results. You are the most powerful force in the lives of your associates. If you accept that heavy responsibility, then remember that your love of them will be the best guide for your actions. It will help you to make tough choices between concern for your organization's goals and concern for an associate. There is no greater challenge than to maintain that balance. Warren Bennis said it very well: "Ultimately, a leader's ability to galvanize his coworkers resides both in his understanding of himself and in his understanding of his coworker's needs and wants..."[12]

Keep in mind that few people want to fail. Failure is generally the result of misdirected effort by well-intentioned people. A leader's responsibility is to help all associates direct their efforts toward a successful result, rather than wasting their efforts on failure. The best way to accomplish that is to help associates find the answers within themselves. When you order them to act as you direct, you show them success. When you help them to discover their own potential, you show them how to succeed. This commitment is possible only if you have the capacity to love them as human beings who have a right to the dignity that comes from personal achievement.

If You Can't Love, Quit Trying to Be a Leader!

Now the real challenge: should you be a leader? If you look in the mirror and find that you cannot have agape for your associates, then you should stop trying to be a leader. If you conclude that you would rather do it yourself than have the patience that love requires to help others succeed, then quit your job as a leader. If you enjoy your own successful achievement of a task more than helping another succeed at the same task, then leave your current leadership position and get back to doing the task yourself. If you try to fake love, you will be caught. If you try to lead without love, you will fail.

As a leader, you are not alone. If your interest is in being able to do and say whatever you feel, then being a leader is the wrong role for you. You must recognize the impact that you can have on your associates. As Beverly Potter says, "Your own behavior has an impact around you.

Things you do and say (or don't do and don't say) can function as antecedents that evoke—or as consequences that maintain—the behavior of someone else. The more you understand the interrelationships between your behaviors and the behaviors of subordinates, the more you can manage others by managing yourself."[13]

If, on the other hand, you're capable of agape, then you may be ready to become a good leader. True leaders have a greater joy in seeing others succeed than in experiencing their own personal achievement. They enjoy helping others triumph over major obstacles; they love seeing their associates receive awards for success; they get chills when they see a previously unsuccessful associate achieve greatness. Great leaders, like most people, have egos. But their egos are fed by the thrill of having somebody tell them they have done a great job helping somebody else succeed. If that describes you, you are the right person to lead and the rest of this book is designed to help you channel that love into those actions that will make you a great leader.

Self-Love Gives Us Strength and Confidence

The first core leadership principle is that a leader must focus on loving the associates, but if you are to accomplish that, then you must begin with a focus on loving yourself.

Loving ourselves in a healthy way creates a sense of peace with who we are. We know our strengths and weaknesses, our good qualities, and our faults, and we accept them. Indeed, our self-love allows us to forgive ourselves for our failings and allows us to reconcile those failings with our achievements. We are in balance because we are able to look past our human characteristics and accept ourselves as we are. Consider John Gardner's advice on how to renew yourself: "For self-renewing men and women the development of their own potentials and the process of self-discovery never end. It is a sad but unarguable fact that most people go through their lives only partially aware of the full range of their abilities."[14]

This love of self must not be confused with arrogance or conceit. Self-love allows us to recognize our human frailty and the need to constantly attempt to improve. At the same time, it allows us to accept our self as we find it. This self-acceptance allows us to be at peace with our existence and allows us to avoid the terrible pitfalls of self-pity, self-anger, and other self-inflicted wounds that invariably impact the way we relate to the rest of the world. For example, if you compare your knowledge, skills, and capabilities to others', you are likely to find an associate who outshines you in one or all of those categories. If you do not love yourself, you will probably be angry at yourself for being less capable than the individual you used as a benchmark comparison. That anger will eat away at your own self-concept and, in all likelihood, will be directed at the benchmark individual. Hence, not loving yourself can ultimately cause you to be unable to love your associates.

After considering whether you love yourself, you must ask whether your associates love you. Put yourself in their shoes and ask the question "If I were my leader, would I love the leader?" That takes a bit of objectivity and a great deal of honest, candid thinking on your part. Take the last week's worth of interactions with your team members and try to think through how you would have reacted to a boss who did what you did. Did you empathize at the right time? Did you criticize without constructive purpose? Did you listen to a complaint and then help the associate? Did you set an example in a time of crisis? Did you back off when you were wrong, or did you continue to try to prove you were right? In short, do you like the boss you see when you look in the mirror?

Of course, you can also go to your associates and attempt to determine directly from them how they feel. Such a poll can be very difficult to do on your own, but many organizations do climate or employee surveys with the objective of gaining a greater understanding of how leaders stand with their associates. You probably have experienced one of these in the past. How did you feel about it? Many bosses resist the results; however, they do so at their own peril. Sometimes, these kinds of surveys are the only effective way to get associates to tell you what they think you do not want to hear. Do not let self-absorption blind you from the truth of your associates' feedback.

If you are lucky, your organization has a 360-degree appraisal system where peers and subordinates get the opportunity to give you feedback. If so, treat this as an opportunity, not as a threat. You will be able to learn a great deal about how people perceive you.

Do You Really Love Yourself?

Since we are not therapists, and since self-diagnosis is very difficult, what can we do to determine if we are comfortable with ourselves? Here are some questions you might want to ask yourself. The answers are yours. There are no right answers, no wrong answers.

- When you get up in the morning, are you reluctant to go to work and deal with your associates?
- When you start a conversation with your boss, are you uneasy? Do you look forward to the meeting, or do you put it off until the last minute?
- Do you dislike the feeling you have when your boss challenges an action you have taken?
- When an associate challenges your judgment, do you get defensive and argue with that person even if you know you were wrong?
- When you and your spouse or significant other are out dining and another man or woman looks with interest, does anxiety and even anger well up inside?
- When you look in the mirror, do you dislike what you see?
- When somebody gives you a compliment, do you have a hard time saying thank you?
- Are you jealous of anybody in your family? A friend?
- Do you have trouble being alone?

If you answered "yes" to a majority of these questions, you may love yourself less than you should in order to be an effective leader. You may need help feeling better about you!

Case Study:

Patricia had a bad night, and the morning was starting off even worse. She was not only late for work, but she dreaded her upcoming meeting with her boss at 10 a.m. She knew he was going to criticize her for being behind on her project. Her staff had failed her for months now, but she had yet to figure out what to do to get the project back on track.

Frank, her favorite project leader, fell far behind, and the turnover in his group was terrible. Frank was trying everything but was having no luck with his staff. June, Patricia's least favorite manager, was continuing to annoy her. Every time she tried to get June to take on just a little more responsibility to help Frank complete his project goals, June would respond with negative, complaining feedback. She made statements like, "I am already working sixty hours a week, and I simply cannot handle any more. Why don't you figure out why Frank can't keep up?"

"How dare she try to tell me what I should do?" Patricia then would think to herself, "She has no idea the challenges that Frank has with his project. I am sick of her whining."

Patricia was fed up with the entire project and with managing a bunch of incompetent, lazy people. She thought, "Maybe I ought to fire the entire lot, except for Frank, and start all over. Maybe with a new group of people, I could find at least a couple with the smarts and the drive to get quality work done." Then she thought, "That may be the only way I am going to get my boss off my back also. If I just get rid of these people in my group, maybe my boss will give me a little more time. I'll bet I can buy at least three more weeks if I look like I am being decisive."

Patricia left work that night feeling very good. She went out with a group of friends from work, and they all told her they thought she was in trouble with her boss. To them the solution was easy: just get back on schedule. Patricia did not share with them her own strategy. She was convinced they would tell her she was being too tough, but there was no doubt in her mind she needed to get rid of the people she did not like and build a loyal staff of people just like Frank.

After carrying out the tough action she planned, Patricia felt great about her position in the company. She knew it was only a matter of time before her new staff would bail her out of the project. However, when she told her boss what she had done, he clearly was not happy with her decision. Pat was fired that same afternoon.

Where did Patricia go wrong?

Patricia's loyalty to Frank, despite his poor performance, was based on the fact that she liked him. Although we don't know her reasons, Patricia didn't like June, a good performer. The root of Patricia's problems is leader "like bias." If she had loved her project leader, she would have had an unbiased view of her team based on their individual performances. She would have seen that Frank was failing, most likely well before it became a crisis.

Making excuses for Frank, and asking others to pick up the slack for him, was absolutely the wrong thing for Patricia to do. In her capacity as leader, it was Patricia's responsibility to talk with Frank about the fact he wasn't meeting expectations and to find ways in which she could help him improve his performance. June was right on target when she asked Patricia, "Why don't you figure out why Frank can't keep up?" Clearly Patricia's "like bias" prevented her from performing as an effective leader. She failed Frank, June, and the entire team because she didn't love them. Until Patricia learns to overcome her biases and truly love each one of her associates, she should not be a leader because she will continue to fail.

CHAPTER TWO

EXPECTATIONS—Setting the Bar Sets the Tone

"How was I supposed to know what you wanted? What do you think I am, a mind reader?" Have you ever asked these questions? Has anybody who works for you asked them? Questions like these raise the issue of expectations. This element of leadership is where the real work begins.

Setting expectations is the first step on a leader's journey. From this action, all other actions flow as natural next steps. Where love sets the tone for the leadership relationship, expectations set the focus for achieving future successes. Setting expectations means taking several specific actions, all of which are critical to the success of a leader and, in turn, the organization. These include establishing a vision, a mission, a set of core values or principles, a strategy, goals, specific objectives, and detailed action plans. Many management books cover these steps. However, since leaders frequently must follow a business plan somebody else wrote, this book concentrates on actions you can take right now in your leadership role to establish expectations that are aligned with the rest of the organization.

Your goal should be to determine tasks you must execute to achieve peak performance. In short, as Dr. Thomas Gordon says, "An effective leader cannot be only a 'human relations specialist' (meeting members' needs) nor only a 'productivity specialist' (meeting organizational needs). He or she must be both."[15]

Most organizations have goals and objectives. Some may be vague; others may be well-thought-out and focused. Whatever the case, leaders must expect that these goals will set their day-to-day agendas.

The Chief Executive Starts the Cascade of Expectations

If you are the CEO of your organization, your challenge for expectations is quite different from the challenges of those who work for you. Your focus will be on the broad guiding framework that is often referred to as "vision." This visioning process is an essential element of any successful organization that is "Built to Last" or tracking from "Good to Great."

The top leader in an organization must assume full responsibility for the entirety of the organization's aspirations and expectations. Most successful organizations have some repository of documents that outline the critical aspects of the enterprise-level expectations. These expectations are typically the mission, vision, values, goals, and strategies that will guide the enterprise-wide efforts. Much has been written about these in the literature of management, so we will not belabor the subject. On the other hand, these do set the tone for an organization and, most important, are the framework upon which all the subordinate leaders build their expectations.

When focusing on organizational expectations, there are a few core concepts to keep in mind. Although much of what the "non-CEO leader" does is to execute the overarching plans of the organization, it is crucial that those leaders understand and accept the core overarching guidance from the top leadership.

The high-performance organization will always have a clear view of its aspirations. Aspirations are those statements of objectives that suggest what the organization wants to be or to be perceived to be. They tend to be very long term, and they tend to reflect ideals. As an example, an organization might aspire to be the most admired company in its industry, or it might aspire to be the most profitable company that also is known for its commitment to the community. These aspirations often reflect a coalescing of a variety of values held by the stakeholders.

Just below aspirations in the hierarchy of thought is the vision of the organization. Here, the leader of the organization focuses on what he wants the organization to be in its future state. This vision is more about the actual business than it is about perceptions of the business by the stakeholders. The vision of an organization might be that the company will be the undisputed leader in research and development, allowing it to be a key innovator in its industry. Or, the vision might be to be number one or number two in each market it serves, or to be the premier provider of insurance services to the consumer markets in the United States. The vision is usually long term and is usually a challenge to the organization to reach a specific long-term goal.

Organizations must have an identity—that is, they must know what they do. That is what the mission is. It is a definition of what it is the organization does to serve its customers and how it grows and/or makes money. The mission could be as simple as: we make automobiles for the broad consumer middle market; or it could be as specific as: we make semiconductors for the cell phone and PDA market. It is important because many times organizations get distracted from their core mission and find themselves adrift in so much extraneous activity that they cannot effectively serve the markets they had intended to serve.

If the mission is what we do, then the values reflect how we as an organization behave when we carry out the mission. Many believe that with the right set of values, organizations can rely on those values as the underpinnings for all actions. Values can be as simple as: we will always tell the truth; or we believe that every associate is valuable, and hence, we will assure ourselves that each is evaluated frequently and rewarded according to her ability to contribute. All too many organizations do not take the time to establish clear values, and consequently, the cultures of those organizations are muddled and confused. Values can and will define a culture. So it is essential that the leader take very seriously what value system is required to have a culture that will achieve the goals of the enterprise.

Goals define what we will achieve in the enterprise. These are the drivers for many of the expectations that leaders in the organization will have to execute. They must be clear, achievable, and measurable. More on that later.

Strategy is the pathway for an organization to follow in order to achieve its goals. Strategy is the "how we will get there," while action plans are the "what we will do to get to the goals." Strategy might be that we will have the core competency to innovate so that we are always first to market with new technology; or it could be that we will never be first to market, but we will follow quickly with new products as the competition innovates. The action plans will be the projects or tasks that we will need to do to assure that our organization is capable of following its strategy. The action plans will also be simply what we do to take a new innovative product to market or how we will copy a new product or service when the competition innovates.

The Rest of the Organization Follows and Leads

The non-CEO leaders do not set the vision, strategy, or corporate goals, but they do lead their associates to complete objectives in the work unit. That type of leadership requires helping associates focus on accomplishing tasks and achieving results. Getting the work done within established objectives of quality, cost, and time is the true measure of a leader's success.

Looking back at chapter 1, keep in mind that it is your associates who will be getting direction from you as to the expectations. How you communicate these must be from a position of love of them. If they sense that this is for your benefit only, they will never hear what those expectations are, let alone understand them.

In creating a meaningful set of expectations, a leader must keep in mind that the expectations must match the enterprise's goals, and these goals must be within the unit's range of responsibility. Waste no time dreaming about how the world could be better "if only." Instead, focus on achieving those expectations that reward the organization with peak performance. Set expectations for, or with, your associates that meet the mission of the unit. If you love your associates, that is the only fair thing for them. Letting them hear from you that you believe the expectations are the wrong ones will be devastating to their success and, in turn, to yours.

In addition, setting expectations requires constant diligence. Goals set today may not be enough. New technology or other changes in our fast-paced world may mean that next month or next quarter the unit will face another change in expectations. Hence, working at expectations is not a one-time event.

KEYS TO STRATEGIC THINKING

Ask yourself these questions. If you do not know the answers, ask your boss.

- Does your organization have a vision statement? How about a mission statement? Do you think you need one? Have you made up your own? Does it match what is written by the organization, or have you gone off on your own journey?
- Do you have a clear understanding of the expectations your boss has for your work unit? Make a list of those expectations and explain what may be missing.
- When you set expectations for your staff, how did you decide who got what goals? Did they participate in the goal setting? Should they have been involved?
- When your boss last told you how you were doing, what did he say? Were his expectations being met? If not, why not? If yes, then how did that happen? Did you do the work yourself? Did your staff do it? What is your secret for success in meeting your boss's expectations?
- There are times when we have the ability to do more than is expected of us. Is there anything you think your organization needs that you could be providing? Have you talked to your boss about taking on that responsibility?
- Is there any chance your boss already thinks you are doing something to achieve that result? Could he have hidden expectations of you that you were not assigned in your formal goal-setting process with your boss?
- What is the relationship between the expectations you have for your staff and those your boss has for you? If your staff meets your expectations, will you impress your boss? If not, why not? Is there anything you can do to make your expectations of your staff more closely aligned to what your boss expects of your unit?

When setting expectations, seven key components will help you achieve peak performance:

1. *Simplicity*
2. *Specificity*
3. *Measurability*
4. *Buy-in*
5. *Team commitment to common expectations*
6. *Self-interest*
7. *Raising the bar*

Simple Is Better

Remember the old saying "If you have no goal and plan, any road will get you to where you are going"? That is precisely why we must know our boss's expectations of us and, in turn, why our associates must know our expectations of them. The best way to do this is the simple way. Keeping expectations simple means that neither we nor any of our associates need an infallible memory for details. A few key goals, objectives, or action plans are all we need to be certain every associate has a clear understanding of what we expect of the organizational unit and, most important, what is expected of them to achieve the unit goals. Remember, expectations are set so the leader and the associates can achieve the organization's goals.

A few key elements done well can make you a successful leader. The same premise drives the ten LEADERSHIP principles. This idea has nothing to do with intelligence. It has everything to do with focus. Every great leader's story tells how a simple strategy, simple plans, and simple execution won the day. Doing a few jobs better than anybody else is what makes McDonald's, Starbucks, and Southwest Airlines so successful. True genius makes the most complex simple. Einstein wrote $E = mc^2$ and changed the world. If that genius can boil his great thought down to a few symbols, we as leaders can boil our thoughts down to a few key words, phrases, or sentences.

BE CLEAR AND SPECIFIC

Which of these expectations is easier to understand, accept, or agree to?

1. We will process all our applications so they are perfect in every respect and so customers will believe we are a caring, committed, and focused company that has their best interests at heart and so that they will always be able to trust us and get a product that satisfies their most critical expectations.

2. We will provide customer delight through processing applications with less than a .0001 percent error rate.

You will probably agree the second sentence is simpler and far more powerful. It may not have the same "good feeling," but it is very specific and very focused on achieving peak performance.

Be Specific

If you were going to launch a business or some other type of enterprise, you would need to start with a vision of what the organization would look like in its prime. It could be "We want to put a PC in every home," or "We want to delight our customers," or "We want to be the largest company in the world." As simple or as grandiose as you choose to make it, this vision statement would reflect what you want to be when you have achieved "perfection." It may or may not be realistic to expect it to be achievable, but it should reflect your highest ideal.

Obviously, the next step is to define the organization's mission. Although the CEO should spearhead the development of the mission statement, making sure the lower organizational levels know and understand their roles in contributing to the organization's mission is a vital part of accomplishing that mission. An enterprise's mission might be "to manufacture parts for the aviation industry" or "to provide accounting services to the small business entrepreneur." A charitable foundation's mission might be "to fund a select group of organizations providing support for battered or abused women."

At a lower organizational level, a leader's mission statement could be "to make the final stamping operation for airframe components" or "to manage the bank reconciliation efforts for all clients" or "to evaluate proposals for seed funding for new projects by existing client organizations." Whatever the level, each unit must understand what it is supposed to do. You, as the department's leader, must either get this information from "above" or set the mission yourself. Then and only then can you proceed effectively to set strategy and goals.

Strategy usually answers the question "How are we going to accomplish the mission?" For a parts manufacturer, the answer could be using modern flow manufacturing techniques that minimize inventory requirements. For an accounting service, it could be a marketing concept of selling only to franchisees of major chains. For a not-for-profit, it could be a decision to solicit funds from people who have just sold an initial public offering and have dramatically appreciated stock that could be donated through a vehicle that offers tax advantages. Whatever the strategy, or strategies, the statement probably needs to be a way of doing something, not a specific set of tasks to do.

For a non-CEO leader, the strategy concept is a little less helpful but may still apply in some instances. A manufacturing section leader might focus on reducing rework; an accounting supervisor might try to develop a system to ensure that automated account reconciliation on all accounts exceeds a predetermined size. In the case of a proposal section manager for a consulting firm, the strategy might focus on finding ways to identify key factors that impact the customer/prospect's decision. As you can see, these are all concepts of how to approach the mission, not specific actions.

WHAT DOES AN EXPECTATION LOOK LIKE?

Anything your staff routinely does to achieve the goals of the enterprise is a potential area for setting expectations. Do not set expectations for tasks that will not contribute directly to your unit's success.

Below are some examples of tasks for which you should establish expectations:

Number of tax returns completed per day
Customers serviced per day
Errors made per hour
Applications processed per day
Parts produced per hour
Lawns cut per day
Incoming phone calls handled per hour
Sales made per month
Cars repaired per day
Lines of code written per hour
Haircuts completed per hour
Accounts reconciled per hour
Complaints handled per hour
Prescriptions filled per day
Orders processed per hour
Applications processed per hour
Complaints resolved per hour

The Devil Is in the Details—Measurement Matters

Vision and strategy are generally in the province of top management, but for leaders at any level the key words are *goals*, *objectives*, and *action_plans*. Detail is king. Virtually everybody is involved in setting expectations. At this level, we must establish very specific tasks we think must be done in order to accomplish the organizational mission. For a CEO, the task could be achieving a 25 percent sales growth. For a leader in charge of sales, that goal could be further refined: to call on thirty prospects a month, or to sign up at least two new customers per month who order at least $100,000 in new parts. For a section supervisor in a manufacturing plant, the goal could be to produce an average of 500 airfoils per day, with a less than .005 percent rework rate, at a cost of less than $35 per unit, and with 99.9 percent delivered by the committed delivery date. For an office manager, the goal might be to have all current-day documents filed by the end of each working day.

Setting these kinds of very specific, detailed, and measurable goals and objectives is the essence of successful leadership. Ambiguous expectations create ambiguous results. If expectations are not measurable, everybody can claim that an objective has been met no matter what the result. If you truly love your staff, you will not curse them with ambiguity, because ambiguity is almost certainly going to lead to the wrong results. By not showing love and not being clear about the expectations because you do not want to offend your associates, you will curse them with an inability to know what is expected of them. Ultimately, they will fail to meet your expectations, and you will have failed them, rather than they having failed you.

The final component of setting expectations is determining how to evaluate performance against expectations. Chapter 5 will present more about evaluation, but the process begins with setting expectations. Your goal is to be certain to eliminate ambiguity early, since ambiguity will be painfully obvious in the evaluations that follow later.

The standard advice on this point is to set goals, objectives, and action plans that can be measured quantitatively. The practical reality is this: many expectations, particularly behavior-related expectations, are especially difficult to quantify.

Make certain when you set expectations that you have already decided how you are going to measure the performance. Many times after a decision to measure an expectation has been implemented, it is discovered that measuring the expectation is too time-consuming, too costly, or too inaccurate. In such cases, you will spend more time measuring the results than you do actually achieving the results. Always make sure the measurement is easy and obvious. If your staff thinks the results may be disputed, then you can be certain they will be.

SET EXPECTATIONS THAT ARE SPECIFIC, MEASURABLE, AND UNAMBIGUOUS!

Using some of the examples from an earlier tip, here are some thoughts about how to make the goals specific, measurable, and effective:

Non-profit fund-raising results. Each development officer will raise $300,000 during the fiscal year.

Tax returns prepared. Each accountant will complete an average of ten tax returns per day during the tax season.

Customers serviced. During each quarter, every branch customer service representative will process to completion an average of twenty-five walk-in customers per day with an average score of "highly satisfied" on the customer satisfaction survey.

Errors made. Each machine in the production unit will produce at an average reject rate of not greater than .005 percent.

Sales calls made. Each salesperson will make a minimum of 250 calls to prospects from the lead list the corporate office provides.

Haircuts completed. Each stylist, each week, will complete an average of 2.7 cuts per hour with a redo rate of not greater than .5 percent.

Orders processed. Each processor will process to shipping a minimum of 99 percent of all orders received in a day.

The best advice is to make an effort to find an easy yet meaningful way to quantify the metric. If a metric comes to mind quickly, then use it. If the goal is more qualitative than quantitative, then forget about measuring it. But remember, without a measure you make your job much harder when you get to the evaluation stage, and you make developing an associate's core abilities more difficult as well.

Again, leaders must know what is expected and, in turn, must be certain their associates know what is expected of them. If associates do not know the expectations, then they will set their own. If they set their own, they are not necessarily responding to the organization's goals; they are more likely responding to their own goals. When the time comes to evaluate performance, then no standard will apply. Having associates guess at what is expected is absurd. It is our duty as leaders to assure their goals coincide with the organization's.

Buy-In

The issue of "buy-in," or assent, has been a hot topic in business for many years. Your success is largely dependent on how well you get that buy-in, but it is also important not to waste your time. Any idea that you take to your staff will almost always meet with some resistance. You need to be ready for that. Also be prepared for the possibility that, no matter what you say, no matter how persuasive you and others may be, you will not get agreement from every member of the staff to a new idea or a new expectation. You may want agreement, but you should be prepared to settle for less than 100 percent buy-in. Think about the process this way:

1. <u>Understanding</u> is when associates have no questions about the expectation. They know what it is, what it means, what they are expected to do, and what it will take to achieve results that meet the expectation.

2. <u>Acceptance</u> is when staff members have concluded that an expectation can be used to determine success and that you and the organization have the right to establish the expectation. They will not fight the expectation and will work to meet it.

3. <u>Agreement</u> is when staff members understand, accept, and also agree with the expectation. In short, they believe it is the correct measure of performance.

PRACTICE UNDERSTANDING, ACCEPTANCE, AND AGREEMENT

You must make certain your associates know what is expected and what they need to do to achieve success. Buy-in is only possible when clarity exists. Ask yourself these questions to be certain your associates understand. Remember, understanding is an essential first step to acceptance.

- Pick the one subordinate who has been achieving the least and identify the expectations you have set for that person. Does she know precisely what you expect? If not, did you make the goals clear? Are they written down?

- Pick the best subordinate you have and write down the expectations she has most effectively achieved. How do you know the performance is effective? What is the measurement you used? Does the associate really understand? If so, what did you do or say differently compared to the associate who does not understand?

- You probably have some personal tasks that contribute to the unit's results. How much of the performance of your work unit is completely tied to your personal performance? Is there an associate who should be doing the job but is not because that associate does not understand or accept your assignment? Have you explained his need to accept that assignment?

- Most leaders have a secret wish such as, "If only Joe could do that." Do you have such a secret wish? What has kept you from expecting Joe to accomplish that goal? What can you do to get that task assigned to Joe and accomplished effectively? Does Joe understand his assignment?

- Do all members of your work unit have a clear set of expectations? Do they understand and accept the expectations, or have you failed to effectively communicate them? Make a list of each person who may not know what the expectations are for his or her job and create a list of individual expectations. Once you have completed that list, what do you plan to do with it?

No doubt, the ideal level of buy-in is agreement, but if you only get acceptance, take it and move on. What you have gotten is recognition that the expectation works, even though the staff members would not have chosen it. In the long run, if the expectation is fair, staff members will probably begin to agree. Save your powers of persuasion for another day and another issue.

Great Teams Have Common Expectations of Members

As a leader you must communicate yet another type of expectation to your associates—what you expect of them as members of the organization. You must make certain each person in your organization knows what the rules are for being part of the team. These rules could be as simple as "be at work on time every day" or as complex as "we expect every person to hit a specific quality standard for output, a certain volume standard for productivity, and a certain cleanliness standard at the workstation."

It is essential that all team members remember this: a team works together, and individuals must bend to the team's benefit. Norm Augustine talks about working for the good of the team: "*Teamwork* is the fabric of effective business organizations. Soloists are inspiring in opera and perhaps even in small entrepreneurial ventures, but there is no place for them in large corporations. This is most assuredly not to say there is no place for the individualist, only that it is necessary for members of the team to be willing to suppress individual desires for the overall good of the team."[16]

Team rules could include clear statements of expectations about integrity, courtesy, team participation, safety, and a host of other traits that set the tone for everyday activity. Associates need to know how you expect them to deal with conflict, what you expect from group discussions, or how you expect them to share feedback with each other. In short, they need to know how you expect the team to work together as a work unit.

Self-Interest—What's in It for Me?

Is self-interest consistent with being a loving leader? Can you put your self-interest over the interest of the team? Obviously, if you truly love the members of your team, then it is hard to imagine that you would allow yourself to put your interests above theirs. That said, most leaders like to envision the day when they are promoted. You would be quite unusual if you did not have those visions of your future.

Keep in mind your staff members are probably not trying to get you a promotion. If they think you are a great leader, they probably would prefer you to stay right where you are. If they don't, they probably would like to see you fired. Even if they think you are the best boss they've ever had, your success is not likely to be their highest priority.

Actually, they probably want a promotion themselves. It's not that all of your staff members are self-centered and uncaring. They are looking forward to their own future, even if that means next week. Whatever your expectations of them, they are not likely to try to achieve those expectations just because it will make you look good or make the company beat the competition. They are much more likely to try to achieve organizational peak performance expectations or goals if they find a way to achieve their own personal goals simultaneously. They are probably much more interested in what they will get from the organization's success. That is fine as long as the organization wins as well. Hence, when you set expectations, make certain that staff members know what it means to them if they achieve the standard.

Imagine what your staff members might be thinking: If meeting the expectation means I am forced to work ten hours of overtime a week, then that may be very tough for me. Why should I do that if I cannot see why it is good for me as well? It may mean I get a chance to keep my job; it may mean that I will get some overtime pay; or it may mean all I get is tired.

"What is in it for me?" is a natural question, and you must be able to answer it. Leaders must use the staff members' self-interest to the organization's advantage. When individuals focus on efforts that satisfy self-interest, while at the same time supporting productive team results, the individual, the team, and the entire organization wins.

Raising the Bar

Setting expectations that raise the bar from previous performance levels is an essential part of achieving peak performance. Seldom have organizations reached the highest level of success with complacency. The level of performance that is viewed as peak performance is not achieved by holding on to existing success. Peak performance is only possible when the leader reaches higher. No organization can survive if it attempts to maintain the status quo. You must constantly be looking for opportunities to "raise the bar." If you truly love your staff, you will continue to raise the bar, because that is the only way to help them achieve their fullest potential. Obviously, at some point the bar can get too high, but you are likely to know that result when you achieve it. That is the point where you will know that you and the team have achieved excellence.

At the same time, as Joe Batten says, "No team ever finishes ahead of its leader. A truly responsive leader must dare to stand out from the crowd."[17] Leaders must set the bar high and must always be striving to increase their own achievement. Leaders cannot set an example that is weak or easy. It is up to you to set the bar high for yourself as well.

These efforts must be focused on challenging associates to stretch to that next level, which is just slightly higher. Incremental improvement is the only useful approach. One small step achieved encourages another. On the other hand, pushing too hard and reaching too high can create frustration and new barriers to achievement. Balance is crucial.

How <u>Not</u> to Raise the Bar

The following exchange between a leader and an associate illustrates the pain that results from trying to raise the bar too much and too fast. Once you go too far, the resistance can get so severe that almost anything you say can be countered with a refusal to try. Ask for too much and you may get nothing.

LEADER: I've set a new expectation of our productivity standard for a processor from ten files a day to twenty-five.
ASSOCIATE: But we've done ten files a day for the last five years ... how is that increase possible?
LEADER: We have a new process that we believe will help increase productivity.
ASSOCIATE: But why change it now before we know about the process?
LEADER: I want to give you a new challenge so we can take advantage of the gains.
ASSOCIATE: But why should I increase output by that much?
LEADER: Because the company needs to increase its productivity.
ASSOCIATE: Why do I care about that?
LEADER: Company profits will make us all better off.
ASSOCIATE: How?
LEADER: We will make more money, and there will be more money in profit sharing.
ASSOCIATE: I am not eligible for profit sharing.
LEADER: You will be.
ASSOCIATE: Yes, but not now. What is in it for me today?
LEADER: You get a chance to hit a new goal. The satisfaction of being better is a good reason.
ASSOCIATE: Are you cutting staff and just trying to get me to pick up the slack?
LEADER: No, but we will be able to take on more work with the same staff.
ASSOCIATE: What if we do not get any more work; are you going to cut staff then?
LEADER: We are confident we'll be able to get the greater volumes.
ASSOCIATE: Are you going to pay me more?

LEADER: No, not right now. Meet the new expectations, and you will be more eligible for promotion.

ASSOCIATE: What kind of promotion?

LEADER: Well, I don't have one specifically in mind right now.

ASSOCIATE: Are you going to pay me more money?

LEADER: Not right away. Maybe, if you meet the new expectations.

ASSOCIATE: Maybe? Are you kidding?

There can be no meaningful dialogue on expectations when the leader does not love the recipient of the guidance. This exchange is manipulative, not loving. No loving leader would manipulate an associate. Candor, honesty, and fairness are essential aspects of a loving leader's behavior. Changing the course is tough, but without a loving touch to the relationship, there is no way for the message to take root.

As you can see in this dialogue, the task of setting expectations is not without its risks. Goals are designed to bring about a new course. Seldom does a new direction come easily. As Nicolo Machiavelli said in *The Prince*, "It must be considered that there is nothing more difficult to carry out nor more doubtful of success, nor more dangerous to handle than to initiate a new order of things."[18] It is essential to stay focused and to always keep the reasons for the expectations clearly in mind since the path will not be easy. Peak performance never is.

Set Expectations for Your Life and Career

Personal goal setting is an arduous task and one that is seldom completed. Our life plans are really a work in progress. Many of us at an early age were led, generally in a very sincere and loving way, by goals our parents believed would be best for us. However, along with goals must come the desire to achieve them. Only you can set your personal goals, and they must be a priority for you or they will end up being discarded scraps of paper tossed to the wind.

For some, an obsessive focus on a specific goal is the ticket to success and happiness. To others, obsessive focus, without the flexibility to respond to opportunity and changing personal conditions, is a ticket to frustration. Which applies to you may be a critical question; however, seldom does peak performance—hence, peak career success—occur without an almost obsessive focus on goals the person has set. Reading the biographies of truly remarkable achievers will send one clear message to all who are willing to listen: commitment drives achievement. Make your goals your greatest priority and they will become your greatest joy. If your goals cannot command this level of focus and commitment, then you may have the wrong goals.

Remember, you must always be certain your goals are aligned with those of your organization and, if possible, with those of your boss. Alignment is essential because you cannot afford to go down a path that is out of step with your organization's focus. If you want to be an engineer and you work for an accounting firm, goal congruence will be difficult. If you want to be a CPA (certified public accountant) in the same firm, it is likely you will find goal congruence and even organizational support for your goals. If you are caught in this conflict, solve it. Make certain your job supports your goals. If it does not, change jobs. Your long-term goals must be a priority.

Your Expectations Must Be a Priority for *You*

The process of setting plans for your life is a subject much larger than the few pages we can devote to it. Literally thousands of fine books have been written to help people plan their lives, and I will not try to replicate their wisdom here. The sound advice can be boiled down to many of the same tools organizations use to plan. Here are five elements for a career plan:

1. *SWOT*
2. *Long-term Goals/Objectives*
3. *Strategies*
4. *Tactical Goals*
5. *Action Plans*

SWOT

A SWOT (strengths, weaknesses, opportunities, and threats) analysis forms the basis for a sound plan, whether organizational or individual. Knowing your strengths and weaknesses is essential to making life and career decisions you will actually be able to carry out. Unrealistic goals that assume strengths you do not have can spell disaster. Knowing your life or career opportunities and the threats you face is essential to knowing what the future might hold. It would be foolish to plan to be a leader of a railroad company if you think jobs in that industry are going to disappear, and it might be tragic if you failed to become trained in mathematics and computer science if you thought that is where the preponderance of job growth is going to be. In short, looking at these four factors can help you understand what career might be a correct match for you.

Long-Term Goals

If you do not have a long-term plan, you are making a terrible mistake. You cannot leave the next twenty years of your life to chance. If you do have such a plan, it will force you to take steps to make certain you are ready for the future. You may never achieve the goal you had in mind, but all the evidence points to the theory that if you are focused on it, you have a much better chance of getting there. Once again, if you want to be a CPA, then taking courses in accounting can further that goal. Courses in art history may be fun, or even an important contribution to your general development, but they will probably not help you achieve your career goal of being a professional accountant.

Strategies

Strategies are tough but essential. They will cause you to think about the key decisions you are going to need to make in order to achieve those long-term goals. You may decide a job change is essential; you may decide a major educational enhancement is required; or you may decide to move to another city or state. You may also decide that you will start down a new career path in order to get yourself ready for the next stage of your life.

Tactical Goals

Tactical goals are shorthand for short-term goals—those you are going to set in motion this week, this month, or this year. They can be as complex as "get a new job" or as uncomplicated as "make my sales goal for the month." Whatever the goal, it should not only fit into the larger scheme of your life but also be something you can achieve for your personal benefit and career.

Action Plans

Action plans are what you are going to do today, tomorrow, or next week to achieve those goals, either long- or short-term. This is where the leader in you should shine. You are an action person, and you must achieve these goals.

All of the five steps above suggest you should apply the techniques you use as a leader to help you reach your personal life goals as well. If you do, linking the personal goals with your leadership goals will be much easier.

Your career is yours to accept or to create. You must ignore the conventional wisdom and the conventional view of previous career models. John Kotter, in his book *Leading Change*, suggests:

> For a lot of reasons, many people are still embracing the 20th century career and growth model. Sometimes complacency is the problem. They have been successful, so why change? Sometimes they have no clear vision of the 21st century, and so they don't know how they should change. But often fear is a key issue. They see jobs seeming to disappear all around them. They hear horror stories about people who have been downsized or reengineered out of work. They worry about health insurance and the cost of college for their children. So they don't think about growth. They don't think about personal renewal. They don't think about developing whatever leadership potential they have. Instead they cling defensively to what they currently have. In effect, they embrace the past, not the future.[19]

Case Study

"Kim, I am very concerned about our division's sales," said Carol. "We have been falling well behind, and I think your performance is having a serious impact on the team as a whole. What are you going to do to pick up the pace?"

Kim sat in complete silence for thirty seconds. Finally she said, "I don't understand. I have been on my personal plan for the entire year. How can you suggest I'm the one failing? I'm probably the only one who is going to exceed my previous year's actual sales."

Carol was stunned. Kim's sales were good, but her 10 percent increase simply was not going to be enough. "You know that the plan for this year calls for a 20 percent increase," Carol explained.

"I told you last December that I could not do 20 percent. In fact, I thought the best I could do was 5 percent, but I committed to 10 percent because I wanted to show you I would really push myself," Kim replied. "I never committed to anything near 20 percent."

"I know you *wanted* the goal to be 10 percent," said Carol, "but top management said it needed to be 20 percent, and that is what I committed to. I cannot have a shortfall."*

"How can you tell me, halfway through the year, that my goal is a 20 percent increase? You never told me that. I am very confused and, frankly, angry. I cannot get 20 percent, and you should have known that and told top management. Also, I happen to know that no other salesperson in the division has a goal of anything close to 20 percent."

Whose fault is it that Kim is a "successful failure"?

Kim thought she was doing well by exceeding her sales from the previous year, and yet Carol sees her performance as far below what it should be. This is a classic example of an expectations disconnect. Kim's anger and confusion indicate Carol failed to clearly set and communicate the expectations. If it is true that no other salesperson has a goal of a 20 percent increase, then Carol has failed to communicate her expectations to the entire team. The top management told Carol to raise the bar and increase sales, and she committed to meet their expectations. It was her responsibility to then clearly relay those expectations to her team and to be certain that each person had committed to meet the goal. Carol should have listened to Kim when she said she could only commit to a 10 percent increase and encouraged her to stretch herself. She should have stood by the expectation and motivated Kim to give it her best. Setting expectations requires more than just defining them; leaders must ensure each individual worker commits to and "owns" the expectations.

The fact that half a year passed before the disconnect came to light is further evidence that Carol failed in her leadership duties. Carol should have been monitoring Kim's performance on a regular basis, and thus would have known much sooner that Kim was behind in her goals. If Carol had addressed this issue earlier with Kim, they could have worked together to improve her performance. Perhaps Kim would have refused to accept Carol's expectations, in which case Carol would have had time to determine one of two things: either management was demanding the impossible or Kim simply wasn't willing to work hard enough and should be replaced. The bottom line is that setting expectations and monitoring performance were Carol's responsibility and she neglected it.

CHAPTER THREE

ASSIGNMENT—Square Pegs in Round Holes Never Fit!

Setting expectations lays the groundwork for leading an organization, but having the staff to do the work is essential to getting the job done. In chapter 1, we concluded that love was the emotional and intellectual basis for effective leadership. In chapter 2, we discussed the need to set expectations and focus on the few key components that make up goal setting and action planning. Here, we turn to the people who are going to meet the expectations.

Once you know what needs to be done, you need to be certain you focus on the assignment. Accomplishing the assignment is more complex than putting the right person in the right job. The task requires some due diligence before you can make such critical decisions.

You need to find people who have the same values, abilities, performance, and attitudes you want from your best associate. If you compromise on the quality of your hires, the team will have too many weak people to win the competitive race to excellence. Assigning great people requires discipline and commitment. It also means making tough decisions when a candidate does not measure up. Pick the very best you can find! Nothing is more disastrous to an organization than hiring people who do not measure up. Many times leaders decide that they have a vacancy that must be filled and fill it as quickly as possible. This hiring practice is almost guaranteed to result in a new hire who is fired or quits sometime soon after. Never hire just to fill a job. Learn to fill those jobs with people who are as good as, or better than, your current staff.

How to Find the Best

One of the great challenges in assigning great people is finding them. You cannot pick great hires if you do not have great candidates. Here are some ideas that should help:

➤ Make friends with your in-house recruiter.
➤ Talk to your staff. The best staff prospects can come from friends of your best staff.
➤ Look for people you encounter in retail shops who give you good service.
➤ Talk to your friends about people they know.
➤ Ask people in your family about their friends, but do not hire family members.
➤ Talk to acquaintances from your church, synagogue, or mosque. Their values may be similar to yours.
➤ Ask people you know from service clubs like Rotary and Lions Club.
➤ Join the Chamber of Commerce in your local area; go to the networking meetings.
➤ If you get an interesting résumé, interview the person even if you have no opening.
➤ Look at everybody you meet as a potential associate. In short, you should always be recruiting.

How many times have you hired somebody because you "liked" him or her? Here is where the concept of being a loving leader must prevail. If you love your existing associates, you will not let yourself hire the person you like just because you like him or her. A true loving leader must pick hires because they are competent and have the knowledge, skills, and attitudes that it will take to be successful in the team's workplace.

The case for filling jobs with the right people was never better made than by Jim Collins in his book *Good to Great*. His bus analogy graphically highlights the relationship between the strategic direction and the need for the right people to get the work out:

> The executives who ignited the transformations from good to great did not first figure out where to drive the bus and then get people to take it there. No, they first got the right people on the bus (and the wrong people off the bus) and then figured out where to drive it. They said, in essence, 'Look, I don't really know where we should take this bus. But I know this much: If we get the right people on the bus, the right people in the right seats, and the wrong people off the bus, then we'll figure out how to take it someplace great.'[20]

First Understand the Process

How do you make decisions about assignments? First, you must decide what the job or position really is and how it fits into the work process of your organization. This "systems approach" to evaluating all the jobs in your group is essential if you are to help people achieve the organization's goals. All too often, poor leaders forget that although the end result is essential, the process determines success. For example, a boss who says, "I do not care how you do it, get the backlog out by tomorrow," gives associates great freedom, indeed, license to do whatever they think necessary to take care of the backlog. However, since the instruction makes no reference to the quality of the work, it leaves the associates with far too much freedom to cut corners and to ignore the impact on the unit's other responsibilities, especially to other sections in the company.

How we get the job done does matter. If a process is designed to make each sequential element achieve specific results, then the entire process will be more likely to achieve superior results. Hence, it does matter what the elements are in the system. Leaders must know those elements and continue to improve on their achievement. In short, in order to assign a task, leaders must know if the task is required, why it is required, and what defines effective completion. Lastly, they must know why that accomplishment is essential to the organization's mission.

Ironically, for many leaders, this first step—focusing on assignment—is completely missed. Perhaps it is because the leader's boss said something like, "Do not mess with the system. We have worked for years to get a stable system, and we do not want you to change anything." This situation is not unusual. Inertia is a terrible disease in many organizations.

Other leaders fail to look into the process because it takes so long to do it right or because it's hard work. Much to their chagrin, eventually the cost of avoidance exceeds the cost of commitment.

Whatever the case, leaders must develop a clear knowledge, not just of the process and the jobs within it, but of how their part of the process affects others in the organization. What one associate does will have an influence on the others; similarly, what one unit does will have an influence on the other units in an organization. Your unit must be linked through an effective process to the rest of the organization. Your output must meet the demands of the customer or of other units in the firm. The recipient of your finished product or service is either an external or an internal customer. Be certain the customer gets what is desired and required.

If the process you manage is not functioning properly, if it does not produce the intended result effectively, then it requires mending. A broken process can destroy an organization, but it can also destroy an individual assigned to it. Before you make an assignment, then, consider the human result of failure created by a work process that makes success impossible for any incumbent. Once again, make these decisions with love in mind.

Look at the Job Description

Why create a job description? The staff knows what to do; why waste the time? This is the classic argument against the disciplined effort to organize job requirements. Henry Mintzberg in his classic book on organization made the case for a disciplined process and structure so as to make certain that every staff member knows what to do.

> Standardization of work content is a very tight coordinating mechanism. Firemen cannot stop each time they arrive at a fire to figure out who will attach the hose to the hydrant and who will go up the ladder; similarly, airline pilots must be sure about their landing procedures well in advance of descent.[21]

Once the system or process is understood and once you have determined the process is the correct process, then you, the leader, must know and understand the components of the jobs. For each job, you need to ask questions such as:

- ➤ What actually must be done by the person?
- ➤ Is the work manual, or is it a "knowledge worker" job that requires more to be done in the head than with the hands?
- ➤ What are the working hours of the job?
- ➤ When is the output required?
- ➤ How much am I permitted to pay for the right person?
- ➤ Where does the person need to work: at home or in the office?
- ➤ Is there specific knowledge required?
- ➤ Are there special skills required?

The list goes on and on. This job definition task is generally easier if the organization has made the commitment to write a position description. However, even with a job description, you will probably need to ask many critical questions about each job. Job descriptions have a way of becoming out of date almost the first month after they are written. They may not represent reality even when they are brand new. Only you as the leader can determine what the real job requirements are.

You may have no previous knowledge or experience with the jobs you need to assign. Whether the positions are vacant or not, however, you still must evaluate the jobs for their specific duties and performance requirements. This may be more important when the jobs are filled than when they are vacant. A job filled by the wrong person doing the wrong tasks can be more of a problem than one not filled at all. Each leader must look at each job and understand the nature and requirements of the job. If you are blessed with a great performer in a job, then make certain the incumbent is accomplishing the tasks listed in the job description. Frequently, a great performer will be performing tasks that are not in the job description or doing them very differently from the job description.

Many jobs are created by the person filling them. When we replace a person, we may find the newcomer is failing because the newcomer is only doing the job in the job description, not the job that her predecessor was actually doing. If new associates have this problem, their salvation could be to find the old incumbent and get some counsel. If that is impossible, then they, and you, may need to go back to the process and find out how this job fits into the "bigger picture." This type of exercise should never be foisted on a new associate. It is the leader's duty to resolve the confusion long before the new associate arrives. If you cannot do that, then at least give the newcomer some time and understanding until you both can redefine the job.

Writing a Useful Job Description

Almost every organization has a job description system. However, at times new jobs have not been formally documented. If you have not been provided with a description for a job that falls under your authority, you may have an advantage if you fill the void with your version of the job description.

If you are going to create a job description, here are some simple steps you can follow to make certain both the candidate and you have a clear understanding of what the job is. In addition, this job description assumes you will take the expectations you laid out earlier and translate them into clear criteria that will be used to ultimately make a judgment on performance. It is as simple as A, B, C.

A. Define Expectations

Start first with defining the results required of the job. This takes us back to the expectations we talked about in the previous chapter. You must carefully define what success on the job really means for the associate and the organization. If the job is to process applications for a loan, then what does a "processed loan" really mean? What should it look like? How will you know it is done well? What is the expected quality of the paperwork? How many loans should be accomplished in a day? In short, define the job's expected outputs.

B. Establish the Process

Once you have defined the expectations, then you must specify how that job gets done. This may be the same way it was done before you had the vacancy, or it may be a new way. Do this in a detailed manner so you can also use it as a training document for the new individual. If you know how to draw a flow chart, make one. If you are more comfortable with a step-by-step list of the actions required, do that. Since few jobs have only one task, you will need to make a list for each element of the job. Make certain the list defines clearly what the person will be doing each and every day.

C. List the Requirements

Now define what it takes to be able to do this job. Here you should write down the criteria (knowledge, skills, and attitudes) the applicant must have in order to be successful. If the person needs to be good with numbers and skilled in operating a calculator, then make that clear. If the associate needs no previous knowledge of processing loans, then make that clear as well. In every respect, be very specific about the core requirements any candidate must have in order to be successful.

The Requirements of the Job Versus the Abilities of the Person

Knowing what must be done is only the first step. Knowing what it takes to do a job is the second. The whole process of assigning people to tasks really turns on your ability to pick people with the ability to succeed. Those who have the knowledge, skills, and attitudes to do the tasks the job demands will succeed; those who don't will fail. People may be able to refine their knowledge and skills on the job, but if they come to the position with significant shortages, you will wait a long time to see them meet your expectations. In fact, they may fail first. Richard Fear, in his book *The Evaluation Interview*, writes, "All too many people have been placed in positions that, on the one hand, make relatively little use of their real aptitudes and interests and, on the other hand, make demands upon them in areas where they are the weakest."[22] How right he is.

The same is even truer about attitudes. It's not that you cannot change attitudes, but the journey from weak and negative attitudes to good, strong, and positive attitudes is painful, stressful, and uncertain. When it comes to attitude, don't waste your time playing social worker. If a candidate reflects a negative attitude, then move on. Life as a leader is already a challenge; don't add to it by trying to be a psychotherapist. We will focus more on this topic when we discuss development and evaluation in a later chapter.

How do you determine what the key characteristics of a successful candidate for a job might be? Start with the job's functions. If the job calls for somebody to talk to customers and ask them for personal information, then it is essential the candidate has good communications skills, a capacity for sincerity, and a sensitivity to people's anxieties. If a candidate lacks interpersonal skills or seems introverted, you need to consider another person. If the role requires strong financial analysis skills, then a person with no accounting background and without a strong systematic thought process would probably fail to meet expectations.

Job assignment is the process of matching job requirements with personal abilities. A mismatch is almost always a prescription for disaster. Certainly, some shortcomings may be remedially corrected, but if the core capabilities for accomplishing the job tasks are missing, both you and the candidate will be unsuccessful and unhappy. Do not set up candidates for failure just because you think they are good people. Although positive attitudes are essential, they are not sufficient. Good attitudes can make up for many weaknesses, but they cannot make up for a lack of capabilities.

Skills and core personal competencies matter. Personal characteristics vary greatly, and some of them can be critical to success. Such characteristics may be obvious to all interested parties; others may not. Some examples of what to look for might be:

➤ candidates for an accounting clerk assignment who pay attention to detail and have basic arithmetic skills;
➤ machinist candidates who have steady hands;
➤ purchasing clerk candidates with strong verbal skills and the ability to deal with a broad range of vendor personnel who might be inclined to sell hard;
➤ candidates for customer service representative who can patiently receive insults from irate customers;
➤ bank teller candidates who can add and subtract and have a pleasant demeanor when under stress; or
➤ candidates for systems analyst who have logical, structured thinking skills.

Many of these may seem obvious to some and surprising to others. It is essential that the leader knows and understands how these types of personal characteristics might impact success in any given job.

Once again, Jim Collins makes the point: "It all starts with disciplined people. The transition begins not by trying to discipline the wrong people into the right behaviors, but by getting self-disciplined people on the bus in the first place."[23] Make certain candidates have the right skills and the right attitudes and you have a much better chance of achieving peak performance.

How Do You Look
for the Right Qualities
in a Candidate?

There is no foolproof way to make the right hiring decision. The key is to focus on what really matters, not on questions that are easy to answer.

Do not ask questions that:
- can be answered by reading a résumé or by doing reference checks;
- are illegal by virtue of federal or state statute;
- pose political, philosophical, or religious issues;
- are personal and have nothing to do with how that candidate will do in the work environment; or
- have nothing to do with the candidate's ability or interest in doing the job.

Do ask questions that:
- help you understand what the person has really done in previous jobs, such as, "What were your duties?";
- give you insights about how the applicant responded under specific circumstances, such as, "What did you do when…?";
- reveal accomplishments and how they were measured, such as, "What were the results of…?";
- cause the person to show problem-solving skills, such as, "How would you handle…?";
- prove the candidate's general interests and goals, such as, "What is your career goal in five years?"; and
- probe the candidate's self-awareness, such as, "What are the things you do best? Worst?"

Strong Résumés and Weak Interviews

You should not interview a candidate whose résumé fails to pass the essential criteria test. Once you have established a job's key criteria for education, experience, and results, you should not waver in your commitment to finding a candidate with those characteristics. These résumé essentials are obviously only proxies for the true measure of someone's knowledge and skills, but they are a critical foundation from which to move forward. A candidate will seldom look better than his or her carefully crafted résumé. Compromise at this point will almost certainly lower the bar you have established for the initial filtering process. Keep your expectations high. Do not waste your time interviewing candidates who simply do not meet the job's minimum requirements. Even in the tightest labor markets, capable people are available. Spend your time recruiting them.

One useful technique is to carefully review candidate résumés during the initial sorting process, pick those with the best apparent qualifications, make a short list of candidates to interview, and then put the résumés aside. When the need arises to interview a candidate, avoid rereading the résumé prior to the interview and concentrate your energy on the interview. This focuses your attention on interviewing the person, not the résumé. Obviously, a candidate can mislead or even lie on a résumé; hence, some part of your interview will always be dedicated to pursuing areas you did not fully understand on the résumé as well as areas that might be an opportunity for misstatement or misperception. A résumé can provide a chronology of a candidate's working career, but it can also get in the way of understanding the real essence of the work experience and accomplishments and, perhaps, prevent key insights into the person's knowledge, skills, attitudes, and behaviors.

Résumés tell you what candidates did and seldom indicate clearly how and how well they accomplished the successes they recorded. As an example, if a candidate worked five years as an accounts payable clerk, you really need to know what she did, how her success was measured, and how she achieved success. It is essential to understand how those criteria fit your expectations of the job you are discussing with the candidate. As another example, let's say you are hiring a hair stylist. How did her customers view her performance? How did the stylist generate new customers? What was the stylist's productivity? If you are hiring a lawyer, what is the best way to determine the person's research capabilities? How can you measure client satisfaction? Is the attorney capable of sound analysis completed efficiently? Is the cost of an opinion more than you can charge a client?

Prior behavior is a great predictor of future behavior, so do not let yourself think a person will change once he joins your organization. What you are looking for are behaviors that will help that individual to be successful in the position you need to fill. You are also looking for people who have demonstrated success as defined by the employer. It is essential to make certain those successes match your expectations of the knowledge, skills, and attitudes that the role requires. Remember, you are not doing social work. You want winners, so look for them and hire them when you find them.

A résumé is a statement by a candidate of what he or she thinks you want to know or should know. Sometimes that effort is successful, but many times it is not. Your goal as the interviewer must be to determine the insights you believe are critical to making a judgment about the candidate's ability to fill your needs. Short of mind reading, you have no better way of understanding the candidate's fit with your organization than to spend time probing the candidate's history of accomplishments, learning, and growth potential. That is why the interview really is the most valuable assignment tool you have at your disposal. This applies to internal candidates as well as external. You must always do a legitimate and thorough interview of all candidates, even those you work with every day. Familiarity is no reason to forgo your opportunity to interview candidates.

A résumé provides a wealth of information, but the interview will be the key to your discovery. Andy Grove, in *High Output Management*, summed it up well when he wrote, "The purpose of an interview is to:

Select a good performer, educate him as to who you and the company are, determine if a mutual match exists, and sell him on the job."[24]

Close Your Mouth, Open Your Mind

The most serious mistake in the interview process is for an interviewer to do all of the talking. Indeed, the best interviews are those where the candidate speaks 95 percent of the time or more. "Active listening," a term coined by psychologist Dr. Carl Rogers, is the key to a quality interview. Obviously, the questions are important, but the more critical aspect is the answers. Once you understand an answer, it can often lead to another question that probes a bit further. If you are speaking, then it is very difficult for you to be listening. Unfortunately, all too often when people are listening, they are probably listening to themselves. You already know about yourself. Your goal must be to learn about the candidate.

Close your mouth, open your ears, engage your brain, and then ask a question. Listen to the response, process the answer, and then ask follow-up questions. This is the sequence of activity required for active listening. If you do anything else, you are interviewing yourself. Never underestimate the value of follow-up questions. Do not accept a candidate's "sound bite." You must focus on the details of the answer and on getting both a broad and a deep understanding of how the candidate succeeded in previous work environments. Ask open-ended questions that require real answers from real experiences. Ask questions like, "Give me an example of how you managed your worst customer problem," or, "Tell me about your most challenging experiences during the time you spent at Mega Corporation as a financial analyst," or, "Tell me about your first job and how you interfaced with your first boss."

Vague questions breed vague answers. Never ask a question that allows a candidate to give a theoretical or conceptual answer unless you are looking for critical thinking skills. Questions like, "What is a good employee?" may yield intellectual insight into employee management but will not give you specific insights into a candidate's behavior. Instead you might try something like, "When you last had a fellow associate who was not getting the job done effectively and was getting you and your unit into difficulty with management, how did you handle the problem?" What you want are answers that shed light on what candidates have actually done and how they achieved results. Remember, you are looking for winners, and the only way to find them is to probe for their successes and how they achieved them.

In chapter 1, we described the differences between love and like. That message is a running theme throughout this book, and it has direct application in the interview. You cannot afford to like a candidate. You must always be on guard against strongly liking a résumé before you have the opportunity to interview the candidate. It is very easy to agree to that statement but much harder to walk it out. But you must enter an interview with an open mind. You can't afford not to.

Just as important, you must not allow yourself to be influenced by liking a candidate during your interview. This is even more difficult. We all have had the experience of meeting a person and, within seconds, feeling "chemistry" with that person that seems to establish a bond. Remember, you are hiring the whole person. Liking a candidate can severely constrain the objectivity you need to determine the individual's fit for the specific job, the team, or the corporate world. Certainly, if the chemistry is bad, it may portend a relationship problem in the future. But good chemistry is not a predictor of high-quality job performance. In fact, strong positive chemistry frequently has an adverse impact on a leader's ability to effectively manage an associate. You probably should avoid hiring people you do not like, but do not simply hire all candidates you like, either. Hire those you love because they are humans. Hire those who, through past experiences, have demonstrated they have the knowledge, skills, attitudes, and behaviors they need to help you achieve great results for the organization. Any other reasons should fall way down the list of selection criteria.

CONTROLLING THE INTERVIEW

Most leaders try hard to not appear as a "controlling personality," and that may usually be a good objective. In an interview, however, it is not. You must not allow an applicant to control the interview. This is your time to make a judgment about the applicant, and you need to be on your agenda, not his. Be courteous, but make certain you cover your ground.

* Make certain you have the interview location set up well in advance. Be organized.
* Take applicants to the location and direct their movement. You lead the way.
* Have the environment match your leadership style—informal or formal.
* Tell applicants you will be asking a number of questions first. Their questions come at the end.
* Prepare a list of questions to ask, and ask them.
* Always get an answer to your questions.
* Bore deep—get to the details.
* Focus on listening to the answers. Never let a question go by without a follow-up question.
* Probe behaviors and work experiences. Ask what they did, not how they felt.
* If you pose hypothetical questions, let them have time to think, but not too long.
* Tie your questions to the candidate's résumé. Get examples of what he or she did, how it worked, and why.

Hiring from Within

Entering leadership ranks will quickly put you into the business of assigning staff. If you already have people working for you, when a vacancy comes up in your organization the natural tendency is to fill the job from within. Promoting from within has all of the obvious benefits of offering growth opportunities to existing staff while at the same time allowing you to deal with people you know. Looking outside your own department to elsewhere in the organization usually will provide you with a staff member who's better known and understood than someone outside the organization might be. However, your lack of personal knowledge will still exist. Eventually, you will be relying on an "internal reference." Since the primary reference will probably be a former boss, you can expect the internal source to be more candid than an external source. Obviously, you should also look to other staff members in the organization to help, including the human resources department. Management personnel who have solid objectivity and sound evaluation skills can be very helpful, but you must refine your own interviewing skills so that you can make your own judgments as well.

Keep in mind there are also risks to hiring internally. Some of your staff may be falling short of your expectations. If that is the case, reassigning them is like moving the deck chairs on the *Titanic*—it will not save the sinking ship nor will it help the organization as a whole. Make certain you are not transferring another leader's failures to your department. In addition, the fact that an internal candidate is doing an admirable job in a current assignment could bias your view on the new opportunity. Make the judgment based on the job skills you have concluded are critical for success in the specific position you need to fill and not on how a candidate has performed in another job.

Weak performers cannot be accepted in the long run. If you have internal candidates who have demonstrated the capacity to achieve mediocrity, then you need to consider the merits of new blood. New, aggressive talent added to an established team of slow and mediocre performers can energize the entire team. The impact of new energy can cause a team to find a new life and a new vitality. Of course, the new team member may also be influenced by the lethargic old team and become mediocre, but it is less likely.

Don't Roll the Dice, Luck Is Against You!

How many times have you said, "I really am not happy with this candidate, but I need someone to fill the job, so I am going to roll the dice on this one"? How many times was that a good choice? Probably, if you are truly honest with yourself, the answer will be, "Almost never."

That should be all that is needed to make the point, but it is not. Every manager has made such a bad decision, and unfortunately, most will make it again. Why? The answer is simple: desperation and maybe even a little panic. No advice from this chapter can make a more immediate impact on your success than this: avoid quick fixes in staffing. You would be better off hiring a temporary employee during the time it takes to find a permanent replacement than hiring the wrong candidate. The negative impact of a bad apple on unit morale and organizational achievement can be so severe that the recovery time will far exceed the delay in hiring the right person. Live with the pain in the short run, and avoid the much greater agony of picking the wrong person who ultimately must be fired. Use care and don't take a chance on an obvious misfit.

Assigning a new hire to any job in your organization can seem like a gamble, but you do not need to go outside the organization to find a misfit. The same type of mistake can be made when you promote a person from within the organization to the wrong job. The person, in all likelihood, is one of your better employees, or you would not have taken the risk of the move. All too often, these "misplacements" cost the organization in multiple ways. First, a bad placement can create an incumbent who fails to deliver on organizational goals. Second, the old unit or position loses a good employee. Third, if the old job is vacant for an extended period, the result may be a performance drop. In short, your roll of the dice may create more problems than it solves.

Indeed, a bad placement can negatively affect organizational achievement. The leader also suffers from the misplacement, because the staff will recognize the error and ultimately the leader's credibility will be tainted. Of course, the concern is not for your wounded ego but rather for the impact your credibility has on your staff. All associates in an organization want to have confidence in their leader. When you are a new leader, your staff will start out with a relatively unblemished opinion of your ability to lead. Each error you make demonstrates your humanness; however, too many errors will not be viewed as human frailty but rather begin to look more like ineffectiveness. Of course, no leader can function without errors; however, no leader can afford to make too many mistakes, causing the staff to begin to question his or her ability to lead.

Your people selection skills get the first and most serious scrutiny, because they speak volumes about how you view people and what you expect of the staff. If you think your staff will not notice, think again. Like it or not, as a leader you are always on stage. Every action you take will be evaluated as an indication of your ability. The good news is that if you, on balance, make more good decisions than bad, you are likely to be viewed favorably. The bad news is that you will be judged most harshly on actions that reflect how you feel about people. If your actions in selection and assignment reflect an inability to choose quality people, or people who have the requisite knowledge, skills, and attitudes to deliver on the organization's objectives, then you will eventually lose your following.

Unfortunately, the promoted associate is the person most seriously damaged when we make an assignment error. Having taken a good performer and provided the exhilaration of a promotion, we then put her through the agony of feeling inadequate as she comes to recognize the new job is a bad fit. In a rather brief time, we put this quality person on an emotional rollercoaster and turn a winner into a failure.

This is nothing short of a human crisis for the associate. Now is when love is needed. First, you must recognize the problem quickly, decide if it is a failed assignment, and, if so, reverse the decision quickly. Second, you need to find a way to help the person recover by providing an opportunity for a positive performance experience. Find that person another job that uses her skills rather than her weaknesses. This may be in your department or it may be in another, but do it quickly. Self-esteem is fragile, and your ability to act quickly will reflect your sincere love for the individual and can help to rekindle confidence and a feeling of self-worth. Failure to act appropriately is most certainly going to cause the individual to not only lose self-esteem but also to look for a way to avoid the embarrassment of facing peers who witnessed the failure.

Unless you intervene, the associate is likely to be a casualty to herself and a major loss to the organization. On the other hand, if you have a great fit, then your associate will love the job, and so will you.

Find the Stars

The simple truth about staffing is that if you staff with mediocrity, you will get average performance. If you staff with stars, you will soar, and peak performance will follow. There is no substitute for stars. Organizations with winning performance records have a disproportionate number of stars on the staff. You can too, but it takes discipline and a commitment to never accept average performance when choosing staff. If you want to be a winner, you need to focus on hiring winners. Loyalty to average performers may be honorable, but it is unlikely to create a winning organization. You must love your quality associates enough to make certain that the people who weaken the performance of the team are moved out. We need to love each staff member but not to the exclusion or the detriment of peak performance. You must love your team enough to assign only the best.

Unfortunately, we all have a tendency to get comfortable with average performance. When somebody is meeting expectations, we normally are pleased, yet we should always be striving to improve the existing level of performance. Good enough is *not* good enough. General Electric did not get to be the winner it is by accepting average performance. Toyota did not get to be the quality leader in automobile manufacturing by accepting good-enough cars. Your company or your section cannot excel if its goal is to be average, and when you accept average performance, you communicate to your staff that average is the goal.

Every staff has a person who represents the best performance and another person who represents the worst performance in the group. Even if you think a group overall is above average in performance, somebody is always lagging. The two lessons here are, first, keep the best performer, and second, either help the worst get much better or help the worst leave. Is that cruel? No, it just means setting the bar where stars can make the grade and the average either strive for improvement or drop out. Group performance will attempt to rise to the level of expectations, but if the persons assigned are not of the highest quality, then that journey can be long, painful, and frustrating. Pick the best—leaders model true leadership—and the staff will grow better and better over time.

Obviously, the higher the level of stars you have, the harder it will be to hold on to the talent. That, however, does not mean you will always lose the best. Something about stars causes them to want to be around the best. Even if they have a chance to go to a higher-paying position with a fancier title at another company that has less talented leadership and associates, most stars will opt—assuming you are really leading—to stay with stars like themselves rather than work in an environment that is short on energy and high on mediocrity. Build a team of stars and you will have more fun, they will have more fun, and the organization will outperform its competition. That is what stars are all about—winning.

If you lead a professional staff, then the star is even more important because so much depends on his or her ability as a superior individual performer in a technical specialty. In their book *Aligning the Stars*, Jay Lorsch and Tom Tierney discuss how important the star is to the professional services firm: "Outstanding firms are consistently able to identify, attract, and retain star performers; to keep stars committed to their firm's strategy; to manage stars across geographic distance, business lines, and generations; to govern and lead so that both the organization and its stars prosper and feel rewarded. These capabilities are what give great firms their competitive advantage." [25]

To Find Stars, Do Not Look to the Heavens, Look to the Ground!

The key to having a winning team is having great players. The New York Yankees keep winning because they have stars. Of course, the Yankees' owner pays whatever it takes to get the stars, and most of us do not have that kind of budget. So what we need to do is find stars who do not yet think they should be paid star wages. We need to find a person with raw talent and then find a way to encourage that person to be an outstanding performer. In short, you need to be the talent scout who sees the greatness in a Babe Ruth before Babe hits all those home runs. That takes lots of time and probably some luck; however, the payoff is huge.

Here are some qualities you'll find in the type of person who can become a star in your organization:

* A spectacular academic track record. Intelligence and discipline matter.
* Evidence of the ability to work one or more jobs and go to school full time. This shows a willingness to work hard in order to achieve a goal.
* Great verbal skills. There is almost no job where verbal skills are unimportant.
* A quality résumé that focuses on measurable and quantitative results.
* The ability to write well. Writing well is essential to almost every job.
* Evidence of job change motivated by a lack of challenge. You want commitment to success.
* A person with demonstrated skill and accomplishment in your field. Great experience and success matter.
* Evidence that the candidate's expectations are based in reality but her dreams are high. People who reach and win.
* Behaviors that show a high energy level and enthusiasm. High energy gets the job done.
* Evidence that the person is not satisfied with mediocrity. This defines the star mindset.

Make Certain You Are Assigned to a Job That Allows Achievement

Just as you need to establish a disciplined process for assigning associates to the right job, so must you focus on your own assignment. Nothing is more disabling than a bad assignment. The psychological impacts of job unhappiness are well known and may even be underestimated considering you spend more time working than on any other activity. All work generates some stress, and responsible positions can generate high stress levels. If you are miserable, the added stress misery builds can have a devastating impact on both your mind and your physical health. In other words, it goes well beyond your job performance, though your job performance will certainly be affected.

In the event you are in an incorrect assignment, then you are likely to be damaging your career. Being assigned to the wrong job is no less a problem in your career than it is for your associates in their careers. Always make certain your assignment is a good fit for you. How do you know if an assignment is a good fit? The best way is to know your strengths and weaknesses and how those relate to any given position. This is no simple task. It is not easy for most of us to objectively evaluate ourselves. We either do not want to really know our own weaknesses or we have a tendency to always view our weaknesses as some type of strength.

When you are evaluating whether a new position is a good fit from your perspective, be honest with yourself. If you happen to be impatient, and you know patience is truly a requirement for the job, then do not allow yourself to take on the assignment without understanding how you will deal with this shortcoming. Otherwise, you are likely to find yourself in trouble quickly. The trouble will manifest as a failure to perform or as physical health problems because of the added stress of working at a job that is a bad fit—or both.

Even if you can do the job, you must also consider whether it is one that truly fulfills you. Making the wrong choice in this light may have much fewer disastrous short-term consequences to your career, but it can be terribly stressful nonetheless.

What should you do if you find yourself in a job that is a bad fit? Get out of the mismatch. In the short run, you may be able to do the job, but in the long run, you are probably going to lose the ability to achieve peak performance. Get out while you still are excited about your work. Once your excitement has waned, the boss will notice and you will be at risk of losing your job anyway.

The key point here is to let go of the past. Make certain you are prepared to leave a job that is wrong for you. There is no substitute for job satisfaction from a job that fulfills a long-term goal. As Spencer Johnson says in his best-selling book, *Who Moved My Cheese?*, "The quicker you let go of old cheese, the sooner you find new cheese."[26]

ARE YOU IN THE RIGHT JOB?

To find out if you are in the wrong job, ask these questions. Do you...

* hate to go to work in the morning?
* find Monday to be your worst day of the week? Is Friday your best day?
* dislike your fellow associates?
* dislike your boss?
* get tired during the day?
* wish you could find another job?
* take your break every day at exactly the same time?
* get home totally exhausted and uninterested in talking about work?
* leave work exactly on time every day?
* find every excuse to not go to work?

Case Study

Sarah was about to go home when she saw her boss walking to her desk. This was not what she wanted or needed at the end of a terrible day. She knew Barbara was going to give her another lecture about credit approval processing. Sarah did not need another reminder that she had a bad day. Almost every day had been a bad day in the six months since she took on this new job.

Barbara said, "Sarah, you turned down five more credit applications today that you should have easily approved. Honestly, I do not understand why you cannot get it. You did such a great job as an application processor. This move to credit analyst should have been a snap."

"I don't get it, and that is just the point," Sarah said. "I still do not understand what I am supposed to be doing. I know you have taught me several times, and I have read the book three times. I think I understand it, but when it comes time to complete the numbers analysis, I get confused. I never was very good at math in high school, and some of this stuff I am supposed to do is very hard for me." What Sarah could not bring herself to say was that she really hated working with all of those numbers. When she was processing applications, she loved the work. She loved talking to applicants on the phone, and she loved writing letters to them. Her new work was boring, and worse, she hated not being able to talk to clients anymore. She felt isolated and cut off from people. "If only I could get the same pay but do what I did before," she said.

"Well, I do not think that is possible, Sarah. We promoted you to your current position because we had a crisis opening and because we knew you were ambitious and would work hard to catch on. Were we wrong?"

Sarah thought for a minute and then said, "No, I will work even harder, and I will get it right!" But she knew it was not possible. That was the moment when she decided that she needed to look for a new job. The one she had was making her miserable. She knew the company would easily find another processor who would be willing to take the same chance she did.

Could anybody have predicted that Sarah would perform so poorly?
Sarah performed very well in her previous position and demonstrated ambition, which earned her a promotion. Now she is understandably

miserable in her new job because it does not match her talent or interests. This situation could have been avoided if Barbara and Sarah had thoroughly discussed the new position and the ways in which it differed from the previous one.

Barbara was faced with a "crisis opening" and chose to reward Sarah with a promotion because she had done so well in her old job. Sarah obviously wanted to move up and earn a bigger salary, for which she cannot be faulted. The blame lies primarily with Barbara. If she had fully assessed Sarah's talents and asked her what she liked about her work, Barbara would have known Sarah was not a good fit for the job. A simple question such as "how are you with numbers?" should have led to a dialogue from which Barbara could anticipate Sarah would fail in the new position. Furthermore, if Barbara had explained that the job involved working with numbers and not communicating with the applicants, Sarah would hopefully have determined herself that this job was not a good fit.

CHAPTER FOUR

DEVELOPMENT—The Good Get Better, the Best Excel!

We are about to enter the crucial stage of being a leader where the love concept begins to impact our behavior. Setting expectations and establishing an assignment had much more to do with the job than it did with the person. In this chapter, we will discuss the role of leaders as coaches and mentors. In order to be effective in that role, you will need all the love you can muster. Seldom, if ever, will any associate be perfect in his or her performance. It is that part of the job through which the leader earns her right to be called a leader. It is here that you will need to give of yourself, and love is the only way you can assure that you will do that in a way that creates a constructive learning experience for your associates.

Your associates rely on your commitment to them, and at no time does that commitment get tested, indeed proven, more than when you are focused on development. Your job is to commit time to developing people's abilities. Your "aloha" for them will be tested every single day. Focus on development, and that gamble on a new associate becomes an investment. Fail to commit, and the gamble will frequently result in a loss. Stephen Covey, author of *The Seven Habits of Highly Effective People*, makes the case this way: "The basic role of the leader is to foster mutual respect and build a complementary team where each strength is made productive and each weakness made irrelevant."[27]

The goal of a great leader is to assign great people and give them room. But, "giving them room" does not mean "getting out of their way." Leaders cannot get out of the way, but they must give their staff an opportunity to win based on their own abilities. It is a fine line between allowing staff members to achieve success and giving them so much room they achieve failure instead.

Think about it this way: Some swimming instructors like to use children's natural instincts to teach them how to swim. When young children are thrown into the pool to swim, what is likely to happen? They may panic at first, but then most will begin to paddle doggy style and manage to stay afloat. A small number actually continue to panic, and without help from an adult, a serious situation could develop, even drowning. No responsible adult will allow that to happen; before long, the child will be saved. You must do the same for your staff. If it becomes obvious that a staff member is drowning, you must save him.

Taking the infant example a step further, the doggy paddle may keep a child afloat, but it is still not swimming. Swimming is a skill that must be learned, generally from somebody who knows how to swim. The key skills required for success must also be learned. Talented people will find a way to survive. That, however, is not the goal. You want them to succeed, and sometimes even the strongest doggy paddlers can drown if they do not get help. You must love them enough to allow them to find their way, but also enough to know when to step in and save them from themselves.

Training and development are investments in accomplishing the mission. By training, we usually mean the process of providing structured learning of a specific subject matter. That could be knowledge, skills, or even attitudes. By development, we mean the broader scope of all the actions taken to facilitate an associate's growth. That could be training, but it could also be something as simple and powerful as a comment correcting a mistake. Every interaction a leader has with his associates should be viewed as a developmental action.

Psychiatrist and counselor to many executives Dr. Harry Levinson put it this way: "Has the leader a right to mold and shape? Of what use is aging, experience, and wisdom if not to be the leaven for those who are younger? Of what use is pain if not to teach others to avoid it? The leader not only has the right; if he is leader, he has the obligation."[28]

The best outside hire in the world or the best internal promotion in the world still needs an investment in the person who is to do the work. Organizations invest in machines, computers, desks, and buildings, but all too often they make a trivial investment in the most precious factor of production, and that is people. Think about your own case. When you started either your first job or your last, did you know everything there was to know on the first day of work? Obviously not. So what happened? If you were lucky and worked for the right leader, you learned what you needed to know to do the job, perhaps even well before you started performing the required tasks. If you were even luckier, you learned from the leader each day on the job. If not, you made lots of mistakes and, with some persistence, eventually learned enough to get by. Had the company made an investment in you, you would have been more productive faster.

Development is hard work, and it requires a commitment to take the time and spend the money. It also requires a belief that a better trained and developed associate is a better performer. Once again, love for the individual persists as the driving force. If you really love your associates, you will spend the time to train them so they can learn to be more effective. This is good not only for the organization but also for them. No associate wants to fail; however, few will truly succeed if we do not help them develop.

Most development begins with some type of training session for new associates. Some companies commit a large amount of money and time to formal training classes, usually taught by full-time staff and conducted in formal class settings. These sessions typically are designed to teach technical skills for a specific job and frequently give a general background on the company and its business practices as well. A new employee who receives this type of training is fortunate that his company believes in training and has committed resources to that end.

USE FORMAL TRAINING IN EVEN THE SMALLEST UNIT

An organization, whatever its size, will have some type of formal training experience for new associates. It may be an orientation program, technical training, sales training, or even management training.

Should a leader have a formal training program in his unit? The answer is yes, since a failure to formalize training often suggests that it is <u>un</u>important. We have a tendency to formalize those actions that we think are important. We tend to do tasks informally when we think we may never be required to do them again. When it comes to training, any perception that a new associate will never again be required to act in the manner being taught is dangerous, naïve, and foolish. You will train again, and when you do, you will probably be doing the same training all over again for the next new associate. That suggests structure and, therefore, formality.

"Formal" does not necessarily mean in a classroom, but you should have a preplanned program, a set schedule of events and time frames for the training, a deadline for completion, a set of specific learning outcomes, and a way of assessing if learning has occurred. Testing is the most common way to accomplish assessment.

Some hints for a successful training program include:

* Where possible, the leader should be the trainer. Your success is on the line.

* If you assign the training to another associate, be certain it is somebody who likes doing it.

* If you assign the training to another associate, make certain he is good at it.

* Provide the new associate with a copy of the entire schedule. Emphasize planning early.

* Explain what the expectations are for the associate's learning. Put emphasis on our "E."

Use Formal Training in Even the Smallest Unit (con't)

* Use the three-step rule. You want the associates to remember what they learned, so repeat, repeat!

1. Tell them what you will teach them.
2. Teach them.
3. Tell them what you taught them.

* Teach the concepts first, then the detail. They need to know why and what.
* Test learning; reward success. If something is not learned, teach it again, only differently.
* Have the associate teach you what he learned—it's a great way to test knowledge.
* Use lots of examples and practical exercises. You are not teaching theory; you want results!

On the other hand, many companies provide training to newly assigned staff through on-the-job training (OJT). In this case, the training function is held by the organizational leader or management and training becomes part of the day-to-day work flow. Most people who enter new jobs get most of their training through OJT. OJT proponents argue that the company saves the cost of a big training department. At the same time, new staff members learn from the people who really know how to do the work. Critics argue that too many people who are trained this way do not learn anything but the practices, even errors, of the workers in the field.

OJT Doesn't Mean <u>Omit</u> the Job Training

You report to your new job and find out your training will be right at the job site, not in a classroom. You are excited about learning the new job, especially when you are told that your trainer, Sally, is the most qualified processor in the division. You will be trained by the best. Sally, it turns out, is the woman in the corner with all of those stacks of files on her desk. You go over to introduce yourself and find out Sally is very busy and will get to you just as soon as she finishes her critical processing. After what seems like a very long time, you begin to realize everything on Sally's desk is critical processing and you are going to be on your own for a while.

So goes the experience of most people promised OJT. They start a new job with the promise of full training only to find out they are going to receive on-the-job training. Six weeks later, they find out that in their organization, OJT means *omit* job training. What a tragedy! Not only have the expectations of a new employee been built up and let down, but the new employee probably is forced to learn most of the tasks required on his own. Picking up a little information here and a little there, the new associate spends a great deal of time trying to sort out what is correct and what is just confusion on somebody's part. This clearly wastes a great deal of the new associate's time, but worse still, the rest of the staff is distracted with a barrage of questions—more wasted time. Further, the department probably has huge amounts of rework, correcting the mistakes the new associate made. If the new associate is unlucky enough, the boss will come around and conclude that this new player is a slow learner or a low-potential associate.

Does your organization's training mandate include an on-the-job component? Are you responsible for accomplishing that OJT program? Has everybody in your unit received the required training? If OJT is not a required part of the organization, when was the last time you trained a new associate on the job? Did you make a plan and stick to it? Was it effective? Did the program actually help that associate grow into the job? All of these questions are critical because they focus on your responsibility as a developer. You cannot ignore the critical role you play in the development of your associates, and OJT is the key in many organizations to the successful development of its associates.

Of course, OJT can be a very effective process for training a new person. With strong planning and disciplined follow-up, the process probably is more meaningful for the new associate and more cost-effective for the organization. OJT is a great way to learn. When an organization makes a true mentor out of an outstanding performer and encourages a real-time commitment, training a new associate will support a quality experience that can provide new employees with a great start. Mentors need to be enthusiastic about the mentoring, and they must also fully understand the organization's policies, practices, and procedures, as well as the specific job responsibilities. Further, mentoring requires patience and, yes, love to be effective. Mentors must truly want to help the person learn and be willing to share knowledge. Not all experts are so inclined, but if a mentor is sincere, then the process will work, and work very well.

Problems arise when mentors lack any of these characteristics, and unfortunately, failure is more the rule than the exception. Leaders must be committed to the concept of training. However, the need to get the work out often drives them to neglect effective training. The end result usually is the work gets out today, the crisis continues tomorrow, and the training never happens. Hence, the crisis goes on indefinitely.

There is never any easy or convenient time for training and development, yet it is a must if you are to be an effective leader. Dr. Thomas Gordon says:

> Leaders do a lot of teaching—giving instructions, explaining new policies or procedures, doing on-the-job training. Yet very few leaders have received special training to carry out this important function. They don't appreciate how difficult it is to teach people effectively—it is more complex than most people think.
>
> In the first place, it is not commonly understood how much people resist being placed in the position

of having to learn something new. It's hard work because it requires giving up accustomed ways of doing things and familiar ways of thinking about things. Learning requires change, and change can be disturbing—even threatening at times. Besides, the role of "a learner" in relation to "a teacher" is often felt as demeaning, no doubt because all of us remember being put down, punished, and patronized in school by our teachers. This means that when leaders teach, they must avoid using teaching methods that will make their subordinates feel they're being treated like children.[29]

How you structure the training is critical. The training must be focused on what it takes to be successful. Each training experience must be tailored to the current level of competence of the individual being trained. As difficult as it may be, you must learn what the new associate really knows. Once you have a good sense of the associate's level of knowledge and skill, then you can address the second area of focus. Do you have a list of all the required knowledge, skills, and attitudes that will make each person a fully capable performer? If not, make a list and take the time to check with your associates to make sure you haven't missed anything.

Only now are you ready to design an effective OJT experience. Without those first two steps we discussed, you will lose the advantage of individually tailored OJT. At this point, preparing a training plan for each person who is not fully skilled will be easy and effective. Make certain it is structured along the needs and skills defined. Also make certain you are able to validate the learning. This usually means you are continuously testing the knowledge the individual is absorbing. You can use formal tests or ask informal questions during the training. The bottom line is you must know if the associate is learning.

HAVE YOU MADE THESE OJT MISTAKES?

In spite of the potential positives, many pitfalls can make OJT a disaster. Watch out for statements like these or the result will be a poorly trained associate, probably also with an attitude problem.

* "Here is the Operations Manual. Read this and come back in three days."
* "I do not have time for you today. Go home and come back tomorrow."
* "I just showed you the basics. Now go and read the manual to understand the details."
* "This manual is all wrong. We do it differently."
* "I know what the corporate policy is, but we changed our procedures. Don't tell corporate."
* "Here is a stack of work. Go give it a try."
* "I do not know how to do that, but we can figure it out later."
* "I know that is what Frank said to do, but it is not important enough to do every time."
* "I hate this job, and I cannot believe that you will like it either."
* "We did half of today's training; let's just quit and get back to it tomorrow."
* "I hate training people. I would rather be doing my own job."

Classroom Training: You're Teaching Adults, Not Schoolchildren

At some point, a new associate will probably endure some type of formal classroom training. Although we have said OJT can be quite productive, it is also true that, at times, the nature of the training demands a more intense, disciplined, and controlled environment. A classroom gives the trainer substantial control over the subject matter shared. It provides for the use of professional teaching tools and techniques and allows the organization to be certain all associates are experiencing the same learning outcomes. This is particularly important when the subject matter is complex. Also, by controlling the environment a trainer can increase the efficiency of the learning experience by avoiding the inevitable distractions of getting the work out.

Does your organization have a formal training program for new staff members? Has every staff member in your unit completed that program? If not, why not? If it is because you have failed to get them there because the workload keeps you from releasing them, you are not doing your job. No matter how effective your OJT has been, getting your associates trained in the formal process will be critical to their success.

If you are doing the training, remember that these are adults in the classroom. Adult learners are more impatient with a classroom environment, more challenging of a teacher, more inflexible in their receptivity to new knowledge, and more eager for real-world applicability rather than conceptual background.

Adults have the benefit, and the burden, of life experience. This is why they react the way they do in a classroom. Most have completed all of the formal education they intend to experience. They have added to that learning a set of life experiences that have shaped their frame of reference. For example, someone who has worked as a medical lab technician for ten years has learned a great deal about the technical characteristics of lab work, but many interactions over the years have shaped his view of people. He has learned how people react to the stress of a potentially serious illness, how they react when told good news about a loved one, how his peers react when they are stressed by an exceptionally long day of work, and on and on. Send him to a workshop on how to deal with terminal patients, and he will come to the class with real-life experiences that he will use to evaluate your lesson plan. Even if he is very interested in learning, he will have his own ideas about the subject. You are not dealing with an empty slate; this learner has life experiences to draw upon.

Adult learners will challenge everything an instructor says, not to be recalcitrant, but rather because they have experiences that form the basis for their view of life and living. Every time a trainer provides an insight that goes against their life experiences or the conclusions they have drawn from those experiences, adult learners will feel compelled to challenge the trainer. If an adult has had significant experience, he can become stubborn about learning the concept or the data. When there is a direct contradiction between the lesson and his life experience, the learner is likely to choose the life experience.

This is a critical concept. Adult learners benefit from experience, but they may also be influenced by events that created a mistaken conclusion. A trainer of adults must distinguish between a valid conclusion that results from experience and a conclusion that is flawed. If it is valid, the adult learner may actually contribute important knowledge to the class. If it is flawed, the trainer must find a constructive way to help the associate "unlearn" the conclusion.

Further, no new idea will be accepted as meaningful if it cannot be put to practical use. Tell a lab technician that people are afraid of the needles used to draw blood and you will see a big yawn. Tell the technician that the key to easing that anxiety can be learned from tricks magicians use and something different happens. The learner may challenge the applicability or value of the idea but is likely to listen with interest. Tell the technician that magicians are able to create illusions because they can direct the audience to a distracting event, which allows them to perform the trick, and the technician may now understand the concept. He may recognize that a meaningful distraction, such as shaking the person's arm, could be the way to make a patient more relaxed for the insertion of the needle.

The message here is not that adult learners are stubborn. Quite the contrary, some of the most dedicated learning anywhere happens in an adult classroom, where the learners are truly motivated to absorb the knowledge and skills required to achieve their dreams. These aspirations help stimulate even bigger leaps of growth, personal improvement, and development. Watching a motivated adult learner is a joy, and watching your own associates learn and develop can be a thrill for even the most experienced leader.

Using practical applications of classroom learning is one of the great tools available to trainers working with adults. When in doubt, have adults do practical exercises and encourage them to bring real-life problems from their own jobs to the classroom. In other words, get them involved. Stay away from lectures and trainer-directed "show and tell." Have adult learners do the show and tell. Many times a class can be the better teacher than the trainer. Why let the years of experience in the room go to waste? Harness the experience as a way of helping the group learn. This kind of training requires careful planning and good control, but done well, it is a fantastic way for adults to learn.

How to Interest an Adult Learner

Adult learners can be either the best students or the worst students. In some ways, it will be on your shoulders whether they achieve success.

Avoid the "show and tell" approach typical classroom teachers use. Instead, use the conference method exclusively. This method makes room for a combination of the instructor's traditional "telling" and participative dialogue with the students. It gives adults the opportunity to contribute their life experiences to the learning. All participants can also have practical exercises that reinforce the learning process.

Here are some additional ideas to turn the challenge of training adults into a great opportunity for learning and success:

* Use lots of "practical exercises" that simulate real-life experiences.
* Use real-life, hands-on examples.
* Have students solve a real problem or answer a real inquiry.
* Do not have adult students sit for too long.
* Be prepared to be challenged and to be wrong—and to admit to it.
* Be prepared to be challenged and to be right—gracefully.
* Do not act like a boss. Act like a teacher. Be patient. Not all ideas will sink in quickly.
* Theory is for graduate school. Teach them what they need to do the job.

Although most leaders are not formal trainers, the fact remains that a formal classroom-like setting can often be helpful in developing a work unit's staff. If you are training in a classroom setting with your own work unit, practical exercises are a great way to facilitate learning and at the same time accomplish management tasks. As an example, assume you are trying to teach your staff how to set goals for their work responsibilities. In the closest conference room—after you have taken the time to describe the goal-setting process and explain why setting expectations is so critical to their success—break them up into groups of two or four. Then separate the groups and have all the individuals do goal-setting exercises for their own job. Once they have completed their goals, have each individual present the goals to the other group members for critique. Without a doubt, the group's critiques are likely to be more stringent, yet more acceptable, than your feedback.

Coaching—An Important Process

Remember the old saying "If the student failed to learn, the teacher failed to teach."

The teacher may have the responsibility to assure learning, but the learner must be committed to absorb and understand. The mentor must focus on creating an environment where the learner can find his own way. This is no place for orders. It is a place for coaching.

Coaching is the process of a mentor providing the help required to encourage a learner's discovery. A coach can try to tell a learner what to do, but the skepticism of adult learners inevitably thwarts the process. If we seek to help people learn, we are really providing them with the energy for self-development. If you ever played a sport, you may have experienced the best of what coaching can be. Great coaches train the mind and the body to achieve more than the individual could have imagined. They inspire and they teach. They inspire with energy, enthusiasm, and love. They create an environment where athletes want to achieve. In addition, they teach the necessary skills and help athletes learn how to execute them with precision and excellence. Good coaches love, set expectations, assign talent to the right positions, develop abilities, evaluate performance, provide rewards, and are constantly growing their own competence through self-improvement.

TEACHING AND COACHING, ARE THEY THE SAME?

Teachers can coach and coaches can teach, but they are not doing the same jobs. Teachers tend to focus on knowledge; coaches tend to focus on skills. When we teach people what to do, we are giving them knowledge; when we coach them, we are helping them use that knowledge.

Good coaching means:
* demonstrating how to do a task;
* asking why someone did a task;
* observing what was done and making suggestions for improvement;
* helping with a task when it is too complex;
* praising success;
* encouraging risk-taking;
* providing constructive and corrective feedback;
* teaching facts and knowledge when required;
* supporting failure with solutions;
* answering questions when asked;
* offering help without threat of criticism.

Good coaching is <u>not</u>:
* giving orders;
* giving punishment;
* demanding success;
* giving instructions and walking away;
* withholding support;
* using emotional pressure;
* being intolerant of mistakes.

As a leader, you are asked to lead your staff, all day, every day. Developing your staff's skills is a daily routine, not something that's just done for a couple of hours at the end of the day. Each time you work on a technical task with an associate, that time is an opportunity to coach your staff. Each time associates have a positive experience, it increases the probability they will learn. Each time you pass up an opportunity to help them learn, you have lost ground in the effort to achieve excellence from your staff and to meet or exceed the organization's expectations of your work unit. To lead a peak performance organization, you must commit more time to coaching your staff. Indeed, helping them grow may be your highest priority as a leader. When they grow, your unit's performance will grow and peak performance will be the end result.

With Love, Patience Can Coexist with Persistence

If you are a leader, you probably got the job because you had high standards and expectations of yourself. Those same high standards and expectations probably also made you a leader quickly. Most organizations react very quickly when they find a high-potential, high-energy performer. When you became the leader, you expected, or at least wanted, your staff to go into high gear and follow your example. You probably found they were moving much more slowly and less effectively toward your goals. Impatience set in.

Such is the plight of a strong individual performer promoted to leader. Patience is probably not your strong suit, yet excessive impatience will lead to frustration. If your expectations exceed your staff's abilities, or current level of knowledge and skill development, associates will get frustrated quickly. If this impatience is not addressed through careful development plans, your staff will conclude there is no level of performance that will satisfy you and ultimately they will leave the organization, looking for a more accepting and nurturing boss. Once again, love must guide you. If you do not love your associates enough to have the patience to coach, then you are cheating them and the organization of improved performance. You have an "aloha" obligation to reach out to them, and that means even if you do not "like" them.

Small steps are a critical part of individual development. Small victories are the key to large change. Seldom does the process of human development reflect a dramatic shift from old ignorance to new enlightenment. Most of us learn incrementally and find that our knowledge gains result from adding together small bits of new knowledge. Such must be our approach to the development of raw talent. Each hour of each day should be designed to help your associates grow just one step at a time. Rome was not built in a day, nor was your or the organization's knowledge. It took you time to arrive at your current level; it will take time for your associates to develop as well.

The key to changing behavior—and that is in many ways what you are doing when you focus on developing an associate—is to never let up. Much of the change you are seeking will not occur if you fail to follow-up on the effort. Your first priority must be to take every opportunity to reinforce the behavior you seek and extinguish every behavior you choose to avoid. Your staff will not get the message 100 percent of the time; hence, you must repeat and repeat and repeat. Never assume that a learner has learned. Keep up the focus, the emphasis, and the reinforcement. It will pay off.

Most leaders have experienced a new policy or procedure that affects the job of an associate who has been doing the same tasks the same way for several years. The change probably makes the work much simpler. Yet, the longtime associate, after being trained and instructed to change to the new procedure, simply cannot see its merit. Quickly, it becomes obvious he is not implementing the changes, and the leader begins to get negative feedback on the unit's performance.

Obviously, patience is required, but patience is not enough. If all you do is remain patient, you might wait forever for the change to be effectively implemented. If you order the associate to comply, you are likely to be met with passive resistance that could be devastating to achieving expectations while at the same time creating a serious morale problem. If you fail to implement the change in order to avoid the conflict, you will fail. What you really need is "patient persistence."

Understand the associate's emotional and habitual reluctance to change, but tenaciously focus on making certain that the change occurs.

The key to patient persistence is to stay focused on the goal of implementation while maintaining a softer touch. Empathy for the associate cannot degenerate into sympathy, but you must recognize that his sense of loss of control is a serious problem and must be handled over time. Offer persistent reminders with a sensitive and loving tone in your voice and body language each and every time you have an interaction with that associate. By doing so, you will ultimately convince that person you understand his concerns yet will not give in to his resistance to the change. In addition, frequently sitting down with the associate and going through the changed procedure yourself to learn precisely how it impacts the job will be invaluable. In this scenario, you are part of the process and you can offer examples that benefit from direct knowledge. All but the most recalcitrant associate will get the message and begin the painful process of compliance. If you truly love your associate, patient persistence is easy because you are doing it to help him achieve.

Empowerment and the Ability to Fail

No amount of mentoring, tutoring, or classroom instruction can prepare an associate for the on-the-spot actions that occur every day. Forced to make an immediate decision, an associate can synthesize the bits and pieces of prior training into new knowledge that is practical and sustainable in the daily workplace.

Giving your associates the ability, indeed the authority, to make decisions on their own without consulting a rulebook is a critical component of empowerment. Empowerment does not mean ignoring the rules. Empowerment means authorizing your associate to act in a manner that is in the organization's best interest. You are showing your associates you trust their judgment, indeed love them enough, to consider the same factors and to make much the same decision you would make under similar circumstances. Empowerment is giving authority to act based on trust and love.

Empowerment is a strong vehicle for learning and growth. It is often amazing how well your associates perform when they know the decisions they make are final. If you have hired the right people and taught them well, then they will rise to the occasion. Yes, they will make judgment errors, but more often than not, the lesson and the values you have instilled will carry the day.

WHEN DO YOU EMPOWER YOUR ASSOCIATES TO FAIL?

Leaders cannot sacrifice the unit's mission. How do you use failure to develop the associates who work for you? Use it when the unit's performance is not threatened. Consider the following examples.

* Give a new machinist a task, specify the requirements, let him set up the run, and check the results.
* Give a young accountant an account to reconcile. Then have another associate check it.
* Let a new salesperson handle a prospect all the way through the sales process—when it is not a major sale.
* Allow a new customer service representative to handle all calls during an hour. Monitor the calls and offer feedback.
* Allow a newly trained lawyer to write an entire brief. Then provide an edit and critique.
* Allow a newly licensed and certified hairstylist to handle a customer. Then give a critique.
* Let the new accounts receivable clerk handle all the transactions for a day. Review the work the next day.
* Allow a new teller to handle all the transactions at a window. Check the balancing at the end of the day.

If you hold the associates back by not allowing them the opportunity to succeed or fail, they will never mature to their full potential. The thrill of being the decision-maker helps all of us focus on making correct decisions. With solid development, coaching, and mentoring, associates are prepared for that exhilaration of success. On the other hand, associates not well coached can swing all the way from astounding success to disastrous failure. Empowerment can only happen when development has been thorough.

Allowing your new associates the opportunity to make decisions involves risk. An individual's failure can cause the unit's failure. You will be required to assess when to allow the empowerment to continue and when to rein it in.

Ongoing Development

Not all development should focus on job skills. Personal growth is also important. Encouraging personal growth is not just good for an associate, it is good for the organization. The whole person comes to work each day, and associates who know and understand themselves have more time to know and understand their work. Far too many staff members spend half their lives searching for themselves and the rest of the time just "getting by" at work. An associate cannot be productive if his day is consumed by self-doubt or worry over personal inadequacy. It is not the leader's responsibility to fund such efforts to find inner-confidence, but the leader does have an opportunity to encourage them.

Deciding how to encourage these efforts for personal discovery can be a challenge. On one hand, we must avoid appearing to act like amateur psychologists; on the other, we actually need to do just that. As leaders, we are not therapists helping people work through their personal identity and psychological-well-being issues. We are, however, in many ways diagnosticians. We must be able to recognize psychological challenges that negatively impact an associate's performance. How we use the diagnosis to facilitate resolution of the problem is a sensitive and difficult matter. Once again, it is much easier to be sensitive to the psychology of your associates if you love them enough to probe what makes them "tick."

As a leader you should get all of the professional help you can to facilitate increased wellness of your staff. This is one of those times when consulting with your superior is probably the best advice. If your organization has a human resources department, then go there for counsel. If the problem is important enough, it may be necessary to rely on or establish an organizational process that refers individuals to a therapist, social service agency, or even private-sector support such as a minister or counselor. If you have a relationship with the associate or the associate discusses the problem with you, then you might be able to suggest he or she seek help. It is imperative that you not damage your working relationship by appearing to interfere in the personal life of an associate; hence, getting professional support in handling this type of situation is always the best course of action.

What responsibilities do your staff members have for their own development? Have they created their own development plans? Have you asked them to write out those plans and then commit to accomplishing them? Have you reviewed and approved the plans? How do you decide what extraordinary training or development your staff requires? Do you have those programs already established? If not, you should create a program that can be used as a general development tool for the entire unit, not just one or more staff members.

Your commitment to supporting the continual development of associates should also extend to broadening their knowledge beyond what is required for the day-to-day tasks of the job. A course in art history may have very little to do with your work environment, but it can have everything to do with the development of a person who appreciates aesthetic beauty. In turn, it can influence an employee's ability to appreciate the value of the organization and its support of the arts in the community. The same could be said for a course in biology, which can help an individual appreciate the need to preserve the environment. In turn, it can help that same associate recognize, and even get involved in, the efforts of the organization to preserve the environment at the workplace. In short, seldom does a learning experience go to waste. Organizations should encourage general educational development. Those that can afford the expense should continue to subsidize advanced education as they are able, but they should also encourage learning in any formal or informal setting that helps associates grow.

Don't just *allow* your staff to self-improve, *encourage* it. Expanded knowledge helps your associates grow. On the job, you must allow them to learn tasks they do not need to know. One day, their knowledge may have a profound impact on your ability to fulfill the organization's needs. Today's seemingly extraneous knowledge may lead to tomorrow's promotion from within. Let the B clerk learn about the A clerk's job. Someday you may need another A clerk. The added cost of satisfying the intellectual curiosity of an associate is trivial in comparison to the cost of ignorance.

Just as important, if you believe workplace improvements can and should come from the people in the workplace, then increased knowledge and skills will enhance associates' ability to contribute to employee-driven change through suggestion systems, quality control circles, and other employee participation systems. Harness the power of staff members instead of stifling them. Their growth can enhance the organization's growth.

Do you have a staff member who has received all the training your organization requires but is still not performing to expected levels? What do you think you could do to facilitate a development experience that could make a real difference for that staff member? Why have you not done it? If you could do anything you wanted, how would you develop or train your staff member? Weak performers may well be the result of inadequate training and development. Your weak performers can be a clue to a failure of the development process, and that should be the first place you look for improvement. Create a list of your weakest staff member's shortcomings and create a development plan that will provide the changes required to improve his performance. Compare that plan to the training and development plans already in place. If there is a disconnect, then talk to the training department about the problem.

Continuing growth is essential, even when excellence has been achieved. Keep the pressure on and push your associates to continuously improve. Complacency is a serious problem for a developing associate. The need for continuous improvement is never greater than when the staff members are fully comfortable with their current level of knowledge. As they lose the thrill of growth, they will become bored and may decide to leave to find something more exciting. Those who stay will settle into a comfortable rut, and inevitably their performance will deteriorate, or worse, they will fail. Standing still is not possible. The choice is between moving forward and falling behind.

Focus on the Stars

Your toughest challenge may be to focus your efforts on your strongest associates rather than the weakest. Anyone who loves people is likely to feel a strong desire to provide support to the organization's problematic members. Again, it's tempting to play amateur psychologist or social worker and try to modify behavior. You could spend much of your daily routine focusing on strengthening the weakness points of underperforming staff. You could commit to making them a success. But when you place your focus on helping the weak, you leave the strong to fend for themselves. You cannot allow your love to distract you from loving all your associates. By loving all your associates, you will find that the ones who can benefit most are the ones with the greatest potential. Do not cheat them by assuming that they can make it on their own.

I learned this lesson from a candidate who was vying for a senior management position in my organization. During the interview, I asked him to tell me about a time when he had taken a problem employee and helped that person to become an excellent associate. His answer shocked me. He said he had never been successful in transforming a truly weak employee and that he had never really spent much time trying. Early in his career, his mentor gave him some sage advice. He told him he should spend almost all of his development time—80 percent or more—helping high-potential people become great, leaving weaker associates with the remaining 20 percent of his time.

Since this idea violated everything I then believed about leadership, I did not hire the candidate. As fate would have it, my very next meeting was with a manager who had already taken up much of my time the day before by making a serious managerial mistake. I spent an hour with him explaining why his decision was simply wrong and destructive to the organization, but he could not understand why I was making such a fuss over the issue.

Right after that meeting, my best manager came to me with a problem he needed help with. At this point, I only had five minutes before I had to meet with my boss. By the time he laid out the problem, it was time for me to leave. As I was going out the door, he said to me in a rather frustrated tone, "Gerry, I really needed help, and you couldn't give me five minutes. I guess I'll have to find somebody else to help me."

I knew I had let him down. He was my best manager and deserved better. That night I was forced to look at myself in a very painful way. That first candidate was right about the 80/20 rule with employees. I began to change my thinking about leadership development. This lesson must be remembered if you are going to build an organization committed to peak performance.

This was a tough lesson, and it also drove home the need to embrace completely the love concept. If I had truly been practicing love for my managers, I would have realized that this manager needed me. Indeed, a little careful evaluation of that manager would have reminded me of the fact that he seldom came to me for advice, but when he did, he really was stuck. If I had been thinking of him, instead of myself, that mistake would never have been made.

It is a tough position to be in, but their needs are so much more important than ours. Our associates must find us available with the love that allows us to help them when they need it. With a commitment to help the strong, you will fulfill the true support function that the best really need. The good get better, the best excel.

You are not going to achieve peak performance with a mediocre staff. Your company may be better than another company, or your unit may be better than another unit, but you will not achieve peak performance until stars dominate the staff and you spend time to develop those stars. The key to this concept is a core principle: a star is not always the star performer. A star is a person who has the potential of being the outstanding associate, yet may not have arrived at that achievement level. A star is defined by long-term potential, not by current performance.

Focusing your development efforts on your stars is not an elitist philosophy; it is simply the best use of your time. When you help a star develop to become a star performer, you have not only served yourself well, but you also have served the individual and the organization as a whole. Ten minutes of helping a star to do a better job will pay greater dividends than ten hours with a mediocre or unsatisfactory performer. You should not write off the unsatisfactory performer, but you must make certain that the star gets the benefit of your leadership first. The investment will have a phenomenal return.

Ask yourself which staff member is your potential star. Have you adequately trained that person? Is that person performing at his capability? What could you do to make the person become one of the company's highest performers? Armed with the answers to these questions, sit down with that person and tell him you want to develop a plan for advancing his growth. Give that associate the opportunity to participate in the plan development. You will get his attention, and you may even energize him with your commitment and your love.

Share Your Knowledge: The More <u>They</u> Know, the More <u>You</u> Grow
In order to be a great teacher, a leader must first know how to share. Sharing means being willing to give up exclusive knowledge to associates. For many

leaders, knowledge is power. By not sharing with their associates, they figure, they protect their own position and assure continued job security.

However, as a leader you are the key to the organization's ability to replicate itself. You hold the detailed knowledge about the organization. Your work unit is, by my definition, where the work gets out. It is where the parts are made, the assembly is completed, the research is accomplished, and the breakthrough in new products occurs. Someday you may move on, but if your unit does not have a leader, it will fail the enterprise's core mission.

Indeed, the inevitable result of successful development is that the mentee will no longer need the mentor. Do your job well and you will not be needed. Your entire concept of leadership must include the willingness—indeed the commitment—to train your associates to eventually become leaders. This transfer of leadership is essential for an organization's survival.

Your ability to transfer knowledge to your associates is the true measure of your ability to lead. When they have learned and can function without you, you have liberated them and yourself. You will be free to focus on your own success. However, if you continue to guard your knowledge jealously, you will thwart your own development. This is because only when your organization can succeed without you can you expect to move on to your next assignment.

If you do your job well, you will be growing leaders, not followers. This means as you develop your associates, you are developing your organization's future management. Many leaders fail to develop staff to replace them. The two tragedies of that are (1) we never have anybody to replace us as we look toward our next promotion; (2) they never have the staff to grow their existing responsibilities. A leader who is threatened by followers who become leaders is not a leader for the future. Always be prepared to groom not only your successor but also your boss's successor. Hire and develop people who are better than you think you are. What happens is remarkable. They will bloom, and you will get even better. That is a win-win-win situation. They win, you win, and the organization wins!

FILL HOLES IN YOUR ASSOCIATES' KNOWLEDGE

It is imperative that you teach every associate in your unit how to do his job and do it well. The organization relies on that knowledge. Pass on what you know by making it easy for your staff to learn.

* Do not discourage questions by making fun of ignorance. Remember, you were ignorant once.
* If your associates know what you do, then you will have time for other tasks your boss needs to have done.
* Make it fun for your staff to learn. Reward their learning.
* Most associates want to learn more. Give them new challenges every day.
* Knowledge is power. When your staff knows, they have power, and that increases yours.
* You will never get promoted if you are the sole source of knowledge.

Development: Provide for Your Own Development

Lifelong learning has been a popular concept in academic circles for a long time, yet the reality of its application to the work world has been recent. Too many leaders have completed their formal education and then assumed they knew all they needed to succeed. The 1990s proved otherwise as thousands of employees throughout corporate America found themselves downsized and out-placed. Many of them were highly paid middle managers with knowledge and skills limited largely to what was required by their previous jobs. We are probably going through a similar period during the later part of the first decade in the twenty-first century.

As these leaders found then, and will find to be true again, the pace of change in the world had accelerated to such a phenomenal rate that within a decade they had fallen behind. And the rate of change will continue to accelerate even further. Anybody entering the workforce today will face the prospect of several different careers during a lifetime. This prospect can be either frightening or exciting, depending on how people prepare for the change. Those who choose to be leaders will also need to renew and reinvent themselves several times during their working careers. Lifelong learning is essential to survival in the new millennium.

Individual Development: Improve or Fall Behind!

The Japanese have a word for this concept, *Kaizen*, which means continuous improvement. From Masaaki Imai's book *Kaizen*:

> The essence of Kaizen is simple and straightforward: Kaizen means improvement. Moreover, Kaizen means ongoing improvements involving everyone, including both managers and workers. The Kaizen philosophy assumes that our way of life—be it our working life, our social life, or our home life deserves to be constantly improved.[30]

A commitment to this core principle was the heart of the total quality revolution that swept through the manufacturing sector during the last decade. In the United States, we have almost always had a strong bias toward innovation and breakthrough thinking. No doubt this is at the heart of much of the success we have had in leading the world of change, but the concept of continuous improvement added a significant dimension to the production equation. Instead of a focus on hitting home runs every day, the Kaizen approach calls for tiny little improvements that add up to significant change. When we in the United States began to combine our capacity for innovation with that of continuous improvement, we managed not only to catch up to the Japanese companies, but we began to pass them.

The same concept must hold true for us as individuals. We must continue to focus on major breakthroughs in learning, but we must also deploy continuous improvement through daily learning. The breakthroughs can be as small as completing a single distance learning course online or as large as completing a master's degree program. Continuous learning can be as complex as learning a new processing system being implemented at work or as simple as learning about a new Intel chip that has more processing speed.

New knowledge is essential if we are to keep up with the pace of change, and we must look for it in many different places. By continuously learning, you are investing in yourself. Almost all of us have some type of investment program. We put away capital for the future, and that is a wise move; however, how many of us have a firm plan to invest some of our savings in our own development?

One of the best ways to learn is to take advice—wherever you can get it. The smartest people are always asking questions. We all have something to learn from others. For some, the thought of asking a question is an admission they do not know something. For others, asking a question is the start of an exploration of ideas. Instead of always giving your opinions about issues, try asking others for theirs.

Thinking "outside the box" is a popular concept, but you will probably find it is almost impossible to do alone because sometimes our own minds are the box we are trapped in. It can be extremely useful to have somebody else state a point or ask a question you would not even have thought about.

Find a Mentor, Be a Mentor, and Make Certain There Is Love

The value of mentoring cannot be overstated. Some of my most important learning came from a mentor. One in particular, who happened along at the start of my corporate career, was critical to helping me find my way. He gave me tough jobs, tough advice, tough critiques, and tough rules, but he was kind, warm, and caring. He loved me, and I knew it. He was there when I needed him and was silent when it was best for me to work through the issue on my own. I could ask him for advice, I could argue with him, or I could simply sit and listen while he shared his philosophy of leadership and life. I did not always agree with him; I did not always like what he said; I did not always agree with what he did; but I always loved him as my mentor.

He found a way to cover for me when I made my mistakes. He protected me while at the same time helping me to learn how I could avoid repeating the same mistake. He influenced me and helped me to grow at a rate much faster than I had grown on my own. He pushed me to achieve more than I ever dreamed possible.

I was lucky that my mentor found me, and I made a promise to myself that, whenever I had the chance, I would do for others what he did for me. I never really looked for somebody to mentor; I simply kept my eyes open for unique talent worth investing in. Mentoring takes more than time. I knew my mentor had given a great deal of himself to help me, and I wanted to be certain his investment in me would enable me to help others fulfill their true potential.

Being a mentor is not just psychologically rewarding, it is an enormous growth opportunity as well. When you choose to help another, you will be amazed at how much you learn from your mentee. In the beginning, the relationship that develops is like that of a parent and child, but as the relationship matures, its nature changes until ultimately it is that of adult and adult. When you arrive at this mature stage, you discover the greatest learning occurs for you both. In addition, knowing you have had a material impact on the life of a truly gifted person is rewarding. Continue to search for new mentees and you will be richly rewarded as well.

Take All the Training You Can

Assuming you work for an organization that believes in training, grab all of the training they will fund. If it isn't offered, volunteer to take it. If the training you receive is poor, help the organization make it better. If you work for an organization that pinches pennies on training, then you must either attempt to get the organization to change or change organizations.

The specific type of training you receive at your organization is critical. Some organizations focus on technical training for leaders. If you work for such an organization, then make certain you get all the technical training available. You cannot work in such an organization if the leadership thinks you are not technically competent. Other organizations believe the key skills for their leaders are managerial and/ or administrative. The same core advice holds: get the kind of training the organization wants you to receive.

In any case, you will have to go far beyond organizational training. True, some organizations will pay for part or all of a formal degree program, and some will even send you to a full-time training or educational experience. However, you are still going to need further development. That will be a serious demand on your time. Whether you decide to get a master's degree, professional certification, law degree, or some other advanced recognition, you will need to commit substantial time and financial resources to that effort. Do not hesitate.

Invest in yourself. Even if the organization has a tuition reimbursement program, you will need to spend money and time on this commitment. Most evening master of business administration programs take two or more years of night classes to complete. Make the commitment, not because you are going to get a raise, but because it will help you survive the chaos of a changing world. Indeed, most organizations do not even give adequate recognition for these efforts until well past the time you complete the work.

The credential is not the most critical aspect of a degree program. The value lies in two places: (a) the knowledge, skills, and attitudes gained from the coursework and (b) the colleague contacts made during the program. These contacts may never get you a promotion or a new job, but you will also be learning from them. The dynamics of hearing and seeing people from other organizations are invaluable.

Remember, not all development is schooling and training programs. Just plain reading may be the best way to develop yourself. Read everything and anything you find interesting or useful in your chosen field and elsewhere. If you are in business, read the *Wall Street Journal*, business management books, business magazines, as well as novels and books about technology, the arts, and politics. In short, learn all you can about a wide range of issues that have even a marginal relationship to your work. This breadth of learning will pay dividends as you compete for the next promotion opportunity. It will improve your understanding of the world around you and position you to take on greater responsibilities impacted by more than the immediate work you are currently leading.

Also participate in outside activities such as sports, hobbies, theater, and so on. All of these offer you not only the opportunity to get away from the daily grind of work but also a chance to network with others who might someday be a part of your career life. Volunteer in a variety of organizations and meet people outside of your current career field. Indeed, you may someday discover those contacts can help you to redirect your career. By knowing others, you also get to know other professions as well. All of these activities contribute to your development as a professional and a more complete person.

Case Study

Ralph has been the director of marketing for his company for five years, and until this last year, he was on "a roll." For four years running, he had constructed plans that his team executed magnificently. The company's marketing results were well beyond the competition's, and the growth in sales volumes was leading the company to superior performance by any measure. This year, however, was very different, and Ralph knows his team has let the company down.

The staff experienced significant turnover the previous year, resulting in a team that was less qualified and even less focused on the goals. Ralph had been on the road almost nonstop that year, so the staff was often working without his supervision. Unfortunately, they had not performed well in his absence, and now both Ralph and his boss were unhappy with the results. The pressure towards the end of the year had grown very intense, and Ralph knew the pressure was only going to escalate in the coming year.

The business plan for next year has been "put to bed," and his team knows the numbers are a major stretch and leave no room for error. Ralph has very little confidence they will be able to meet the goals. He is convinced they simply do not have enough experience, know enough about the company, or actually care enough about the goals to achieve success. He is heading into the new year with a feeling of dread that it will be another year of failure.

What can/should Ralph do?

Ralph appears to have accepted little or no responsibility for the failure of his team. Four years of success probably caused him to become overly confident about his own abilities. It sounds like he is setting the goals for his staff but failing to engage them in the process or helping them improve. In addition, he does not seem to understand turnover is both a problem that could be a reflection of his leadership and a problem that could create the failure to perform.

Ralph seems to be aware of the fact that his people may not have the right skills, experience, and attitude, but he is missing the point that these issues are his responsibility, not theirs. Ralph clearly appears to have a leadership problem, and hopefully he will do his own evaluation and come to the same conclusion. It is pretty obvious that previous employees left him for reasons that may have to do with the fact that he was not in the office much and, therefore, not available for nurturing and guidance.

As a practical matter, Ralph needs to have a preliminary session with his staff, followed by a diagnostic with each member, to determine what they need in the way of development efforts. It is critical that Ralph take an honest look at his own leadership activities and determine what he needs to do in order to be the effective, proactive leader he was during the first four years. It is not unusual for leaders to fall into the trap of thinking that once they succeed, that success will continue to happen. Every day must be a point of renewal and re-energizing. That is why, at a minimum, the best leaders use the annual "New Year" to critique themselves and identify where they can improve, or fix their own problematic behaviors. Your staff looks to you for guidance and example, so show them your commitment to improving as you set out the ways in which they can improve.

CHAPTER FIVE

EVALUATION—Leaders Succeed by Making Judgments

A quick review: We started with *love* for our associates, established *expectations*, made the right *assignment*, and then worked at *development*. Most readers would probably guess performance *evaluation* is the logical next step. Yet if it is so obvious, why is evaluation so often ignored, postponed, or forgotten? How many times in your career have you waited a whole year for your annual performance appraisal only to discover you have not been doing the job?

Evaluation Is Hard Work; With Love It Might Be Less Stressful

We have returned to the principle of love many times. However, nowhere is this concept more important than in evaluation, which is often the most personally challenging and potentially painful aspect of being a leader. Nothing you do can be more helpful or damaging to your associates. Do evaluations well and they can be exhilarating for you and your team. Do them poorly and they can be devastating for both. No wonder this step in the ten LEADERSHIP principles is so frequently avoided.

For many leaders, performing evaluations is one of their least enjoyable tasks. Why do so many dislike it? You may say you only have a problem giving evaluations when people are not doing the job.

If that is true, then assuming that only 10 percent or so of associates are failures, does that mean that 90 percent of the time you like doing them? In fact, giving performance reviews to outstanding performers can be just as hard as giving performance reviews to unsatisfactory performers. The truth is they are very hard work.

Ironically, we ourselves want to receive meaningful and timely performance reviews. This is especially true if we think we have done a great job. You would think if it is personally desirable for us to get feedback, then we should want to offer feedback to our associates. Yet the evidence is clear; most leaders would rather work three shifts in a row than have a single negative feedback session with a subordinate.

Five Reasons Why Leaders Avoid Evaluations

For leaders, evaluation is work they know must be done but which they tend to avoid at almost all costs. Leaders find these evaluations tough for several reasons:

1. Most of us simply do not enjoy being judgmental about others, especially people we work with every day. We would like to avoid such conversations because they create tension.

2. We don't want to cope with disagreement from the associate being evaluated. Associates are likely to agree with positive feedback, and they are just as likely to disagree with negative feedback. Most bosses would avoid the conflict if they could, and many do by simply ignoring the evaluation process. The stress is intensified if the performance review is tied to pay, as most often it is. Even an outstanding performer, in a meaningful and honest evaluation, will almost always require some negative feedback. But since we generally do not want to complicate or alienate a positive performance, we often give a performance review that is all positives, with

no negatives. Consequently, we never address the issues that call for action.

3. In order to evaluate, we need criteria. That means we need to have expectations we can compare to the job performance. If we have not made the expectations list specific and measurable, we have a very difficult time measuring against the benchmark. The worse we are at setting expectations, the more we will worry and procrastinate when it comes time for evaluations. Ultimately, the result will be an evaluation that is weak to inadequate, and that compounds the tension that already exists when negative feedback is given.

4. The documentation required for an evaluation takes a lot of time that we would much rather spend getting the work out. Often we are required to complete forms that make us record factors we are not really tracking or that we think are irrelevant. Worse still, we sometimes wish we had focused on those items, but now it is too late, and we are going to have to fake the results.

5. We usually are convinced that the people who are doing a good job know we think they are great and that formal evaluations are a waste of time. We want to tell them "everything is fine" and not much more. We give them no evaluation, just a quick comment and a salary increase. Now everybody is happy and we can go back to work.

The simple fact is all of these reasons reflect a failure to assure performance. Ken Blanchard says it all: "Everyone has peak performance potential. You just need to know where they are coming from and meet them there."[31] The problem is you can never "meet them there" if you never tell them where you are. How can you develop your associates if you never give them insight into their current performance level?

ASK YOURSELF
THESE QUESTIONS

And You'll Remember Why Appraisals Are Tough

- Have you ever been surprised by a remark on your annual performance appraisal? Why? What did you do about it?

- When was the last time you got feedback from your boss? Was it positive feedback? Was it negative? What did you do about the feedback? Did your boss discuss how you could improve?

- Think of your worst staff member. When was the last time you gave that person a formal performance appraisal? When was the last time you actually sat down and discussed performance since that time? What happened?

- Think of your best staff member. When was the last time you gave that person any feedback at all? What was it about? What was the outcome?

- What happened when you had your last performance appraisal with a staff member? What was the result of that meeting? Has there been any change in performance from that person?

If This Were Simple, Then Everybody Would Be a Leader

Giving a performance review to an outstanding performer can really make you feel good. For most of us, praise is a great deal more fun than criticism. It is only when we are forced to give strong, highly critical, and negative feedback that most of us wish we could ask somebody else to do it for us.

One senior executive routinely did just that. He would give all the positive reviews himself and leave the negative reviews, and even firings, to his director of human resources. This man was incapable of facing his responsibilities as a leader. He always wanted to feel good and could not face the difficult task of confronting another human being with the honest and caring truth. Worse still, he convinced many people in the organization he was such a warm and caring person that he could not bring himself to hurt anybody. What a fraud! If he truly loved his associates, he would have recognized it was his duty to do everything he could to help them succeed, even if on occasion that meant telling them something they did not want to hear.

GET YOURSELF READY FOR THAT TOUGH FEEDBACK SESSION

As you prepare yourself for a feedback session, here are some thoughts that might help you keep your resolve:

* Remind yourself that you are a great leader, and great leaders evaluate performance.
* Remember, feedback is part of the job.
* Remember, procrastinating only puts off the inevitable.
* Associate performance must be better or our unit is at risk.
* How can he improve if I do not tell him about the problem?
* She deserves honest feedback for her outstanding performance.
* My other associates deserve better performance from this weaker associate. Feedback may help improve his performance.
* Her behavior is abusive and unacceptable. Tough love may be the only solution.
* This associate is not right for the job. She is probably miserable as well.
* This associate has broken the value of integrity and trust. He should have been terminated yesterday.
* This associate has alienated our customers many times. They pay the bills.
* His performance is negatively impacting the others in the unit.
* I have worked with her for six months, but she has done nothing to improve. Enough is enough.
* I have spent too much time trying to help a hopeless case. Others need my time.

Loving humans requires helping them, even if the truth is painful. People with no understanding of their weaknesses are living in a fantasy world. It is our duty as leaders to help our associates deal with their own shortcomings as well as to understand their strengths. Just as in a manufacturing environment, we can only improve the process by understanding its weaknesses. Improvement cannot happen if we do not know what needs to be improved, and without improvement there can be no excellence.

You will hear this again, but remember that you are not trying to create capability; you are working to enhance it. Do not waste your time on the hopeless, but where there is hope, give it a real commitment. In their book *First, Break All the Rules*, Buckingham and Coffman say it simply: "People don't change that much. Don't waste time trying to put in what was left out. Try to draw what was left in. That is hard enough."[32]

Even Daily Feedback May Be Too Seldom

Compounding the problem of giving effective evaluations is that all too often they are relegated to a once-a-year activity. Nothing could be worse. The practice of waiting a full year to give direct, formal evaluation and performance feedback is unfair to the associate and illogical for the organization's interests. Evaluation must be an activity tied to the individual's daily performance, not to the convenience of a process. We cannot expect associates to know what we do not tell them. Either positive or negative messages about behavior or performance must be communicated at the time of the event, not a month or a year later. How can we expect change if we make no attempt to inform associates about their performance?

Annual reviews do not work to the associate's or the organization's benefit. Over forty years ago, Douglas McGregor, in his classic book *The Human Side of Enterprise*, wrote about the annual performance appraisal. His message is still on the mark:

> The semiannual or annual appraisal is not a particularly efficient stimulus to learning for another reason: It provides "feedback" about behavior at a time remote from the behavior itself. People do learn and change as a result

of feedback. In fact, it is the only way they learn. However, the most effective feedback occurs immediately after the behavior. The subordinate can learn a great deal from a mistake, or a particular failure in a performance, provided it is analyzed while all the evidence is immediately at hand. Three or four months later, the likelihood of effective learning from that experience is small. It will be still smaller if the superior's generalized criticism relates to several incidents spread over a period of months.[33]

GIVE ONE-MINUTE FEEDBACK—IMMEDIATELY

Whenever it is obvious an associate's behavior was either exceptionally good or inappropriate is the right time for one-minute feedback.

Here are some good rules for a one-minute feedback session:
Do it immediately.
Waste no time.
Make your comments clear and crisp.
Be calm and yet firm.
Refer directly to what just happened.
If it is positive feedback, be positive, warm, and friendly.
If it is negative feedback, make it firm but gentle.
Above all, make the session short and focused only on the event, not a history lesson on other events.

A behavioral psychologist, such as B.F. Skinner, would say if you fail to reinforce desired behavior, it will eventually disappear. And if you fail to punish undesirable behavior, you will encourage it to continue. Classical Freudian psychology would hold that behavior will persist until an individual understands the core reasons for its existence. In any case, allowing an associate to continue working without an honest evaluation of behaviors and performances is a classic sign that the leader has failed the love test.

If we really loved our associates, we would not allow them to drift with no idea as to how they stand. Unfortunately, too many of us fail our associates and give them, at best, severely delayed feedback.

Make Certain You Really Have the Associate's Attention

One of the great problems in giving feedback is making certain it is received. Most of us have a difficult time receiving feedback, and when we do, we only listen to what we either believe or want to believe. Further, we all have a tendency to believe only comments that are positive. Think about the last time you were asked to list your strengths and weaknesses. In all likelihood, you did a good job on the strengths and not so well on the weaknesses. The weaknesses you listed were probably qualities you actually considered strengths. Most of us have a difficult time admitting to real weaknesses, and if we do, we generally find a way to excuse them. We tend to do the same with evaluations.

Think about the last time you asked an associate the question "Tell me about your weaknesses." The associate probably answered with comments like "I am impatient when my staff falls short of their goals," or "I set standards that some people think are too high," or "I work too many hours in a day." In all likelihood, the associate really believed these observations could be viewed by some as weaknesses but only if the behavior was extreme. In most cases, impatience is good when it looks for excellence, high standards are great when they challenge associates to achieve excellence, and hard work is a positive when it reflects an associate's commitment to achievement. In short, the comments really reflect pride, not weakness.

In addition, most people have a tendency to block out bad news because they find it much more enjoyable to go through life hearing only good news. Worse still, because people often do not want to face negatives, they hear them but do not process them. Thus, a counseling session by a concerned boss can often be totally lost because the comments are heard but not listened to. The sound hits the eardrum but does not make its way to the conscious mind for processing. How many times have you shut out a speaker's words by simply turning off your attention? Your associates will do the same to you.

EIGHT MORE WAYS TO GET AND KEEP YOUR ASSOCIATES' ATTENTION

Try some of these statements when you need to get an associate's attention.

* To be direct: "Frank, I want you to know this is a formal feedback session."

* For the receptive type: "Joe, I have some thoughts that might help you improve."

* For the chronic failure: "Barb, we have talked about this problem before."

* For the serious event: "John, you just made a serious mistake; let's talk."

* For the worrier: "Sally, you have asked me to give you feedback, well..."

* For the rude one: "Kim, I would like to discuss your outburst."

* For a victory: "Stephen, you just did a great job. Thank you."

* For an obvious error: "Mark, I am very concerned about the way you handled that."

You've likely had a number of associates who received frequent feedback yet later told you they were never told about their failings. Such denials probably frustrated and bewildered you. Try this technique to prevent that scenario. Tell the associate she should listen carefully because you are turning on the counseling switch, at which time you walk over to the light switch on the wall and turn on the bright ceiling lights. This bit of drama often works. By the time you sit down at the table, your associate will be clearly focused on what you have to say. Although a playful approach may not work with all associates, you need to do whatever it takes to get their attention. The "counseling switch" idea works much of the time but not always. Some associates either do not get the idea or are offended by the gamesmanship. Remember, you are leading a team but each member of that team is an individual. Some ideas work with some and not with others. Keep trying. For most people, something will get their attention, but it may not always be obvious. Always use the person's name, and always make the feedback session private. Whatever you do, make certain the associate understands you are serious and expect her attention. When you give feedback, particularly negative feedback, literally announce you are about to begin a counseling session. This suggests that what is about to occur involves the associate's performance and must be remembered.

Talk about Behavior First

We all know that job performance is what we must focus on. Our expectations are the driving force for our leadership position. If our associates' performance is either superior or unsatisfactory, we must offer them feedback. However, we must also understand that all individual performance is a function of behavior. If associates come to the job with severe behavioral limitations, then their job performance will be negative. If they come to the job with certain essential weaknesses that could be improved in order to substantially improve job performance, then we have a duty to provide feedback. It's the duty of a leader, I should say, who truly loves and cares about his or her associates' success.

If what people are and how they behave can make a difference in expectations, then we must, as leaders, focus on those. Qualities like intelligence and the ability to reason, to think logically, to articulate ideas, and to function under stress help to define what people are and how they will perform. So do the capacity to relate to people, the intensity of the work ethic, and much more. You need to know your associates. It is not enough to say, "You did a great job." You need to understand them as whole beings.

A good way to do this is to use "trait reviews." These are not report cards on behavior like children get in elementary school, but they do have one critical resemblance: they give feedback on behavior characteristics that can influence the ability to perform. The goal must be to focus on results, on performance compared to expectations; however, it is equally important to give feedback on traits that either help or hinder success. If an associate has difficulty developing working relationships with her peers, that weakness will have a major influence on her ability to achieve results in almost any organization. Effective feedback, counseling, and developmental support are critical if the associate is going to become a superior performer. If you choose to avoid this sensitive psychological issue, you will cheat the employee of support that could make a huge difference in both current and future assignments. If you really have the capacity to love an associate, you must take on this topic and attempt to help the individual deal with the shortcoming. Of course, how effective you are will depend in large measure on the individual's receptivity; however, your performance is critical also. If you give feedback in a manner sensitive to the recipient's mindset—in other words, if you "walk in her shoes"—you will have a much better chance of being heard and heeded than if you chose to preach and moralize.

Giving speeches may make you feel better, but the tone may also make an associate reject what you say. The associate must acknowledge the weakness and accept it as an issue that requires change. No amount of preaching brings positive change if you alienate the associate. Only when the individual acknowledges the problem can a solution be found and implemented. By the same token, if you never raise the issue because you think psychology is not your role, then you will probably fail to provide your contribution to the development of a superior performer. This part of evaluation is hard work, but it is what leaders must do if they are to play their role well. Helping to make winners is not always easy, but it will always be rewarding for a leader who begins with love.

Trait Reviews Are Tough, But They Can Be Fruitful

A great deal can be gained from taking the time to talk to your associates about how their traits and behaviors affect job performance. The good news is most of the issues you are talking about influence job performance; the bad news is you may misjudge the situation and then have to argue with the associate. In addition, you are doing something that is not normally comfortable: telling people how you perceive them. You will be focusing on insights you have drawn from working with them. You will be talking about them and their behavior, not just their job performance. We think about people's behavior all the time, but seldom do we tell them what we think. Yet results at work are almost always tied to behaviors. You may not be able to change asswociates' behavior, but if they know what you have observed, they may conclude that they must attempt to deal with these issues.

Incidentally, in the event you are challenged on the feedback you offer, here is a simple way to deal with an objection: acknowledge that you know you may be wrong, but that is why you are talking about it. You are trying to get a better understanding of her, so that you both can judge her ability to improve. Tell her you will spend some more time thinking about it. This acknowledges that you could be wrong without saying definitively that you are. Being right is not the issue. Giving the associate this information makes it possible for her to understand the perceptions that exist.

The content of a "trait review" follows a simple structure, but it must always be part of a comprehensive review of the associate's performance. Never do a trait review without tying it to a performance evaluation. The goal is to give associates an opportunity to see that their performance can be tied to their personal traits. Also never tell associates you are evaluating them on their personal traits. Performance evaluations should be based on the associate's achievement of results. But the trait review gives the associate an opportunity to correct issues that affect performance.

The Process Is Critical

Always begin a trait review with an introduction explaining to the associate that you are not a psychologist, but rather a leader who has great interest in understanding her so you can help her grow and improve. Then give a general review of the categories you will discuss and the reasons for discussing them.

I. *The Mind*

Mental skills certainly affect job performance because most jobs today can be viewed as "knowledge worker" positions. How the individual uses mental skills is critical to the ability to learn and execute job functions. In this part of the trait review, give the associate feedback on abilities such as:

    a.   the ability to achieve effective reasoning;

    b.   problem-solving skills;

    c.   systematic and logical thinking;

    d.   the ability to employ analytical skills to create new approaches; and

    e.   the speed with which the associate learns new ideas.

II. *The Emotions*

Emotional stability and control is a critical requirement in any job environment because the individual must be reliable over an extended period of time and in a variety of situations. In this part of the trait review, you will give the associate feedback on characteristics such as:

    a.   the ability to maintain emotional control;

    b.   the ability to deal with constructive feedback on work performance;

    c.   commitment to work;

    d.   self-confidence;

    e.   the ability to deal with change and stressful situations; and

    f.   the ability to avoid personal problems that affect on-the-job performance.

III. *The Knowledge*

Every associate must be able to demonstrate a core knowledge and understanding of the work they are doing. In this part of the trait review, you will give the associate feedback on how you evaluate his or her job knowledge, such as:

    a.   understanding of business principles in general;

    b.   understanding of the specific work unit activities;

    c.   knowledge and understanding of the organization as a whole;

    d.   knowledge of the specific job the associate is assigned to accomplish; and

    e.   the application of knowledge that contributes to required job skills.

IV. *The Relationships*

Any person in the workplace must ultimately deal with co-workers in order to be effective. In this part of the trait review, you will give the associate feedback on abilities such as:

    a.   working with colleagues;

    b.   developing a sound working relationship with you, the boss;

    c.   working as a team member;

    d.   leadership;

    e.   developing cross-organizational relationships; and

    f.   effectively handling customers, vendors, or any other professional relationships that impact the ability to achieve success on the job.

V. *The Future*

Any associate who is to be a star in an organization needs to be able to think about the long run. In this part of the trait review, you will give the associate feedback on abilities such as:

    a.   seeing and understanding business growth opportunities;

    b.   developing plans for improvement in the organization; and

    c.   establishing plans for personal development.

When you take the time to discuss these key characteristics, you demonstrate to an associate you are committed to feedback. By sharing these thoughts, you give associates an opportunity to understand how you perceive them and how you believe others in the organization perceive them.

Love Means Honesty and Candor—Not Brutality

Giving effective feedback is hard work, but taking it is too. Hearing negative words about our behavior or performance is painful. Consequently, when we are in a position to give feedback, we usually attempt to couch the words in the most appealing fashion we can.

If you have been exposed to any formal sales training, you were probably taught you should always deal with negatives in a sales situation by attempting to focus on the positives instead. You were also probably told you must make yourself communicate in a positive fashion in order to get a resistant buyer to buy. In this case, there is no doubt the recipient of constructive feedback in an evaluation session will be a "reluctant buyer." Such training gives you all the more reason to walk carefully through the feedback minefield.

However, providing candid and direct insight is better than trying to mask the truth and spare people the pain of confronting their weaknesses. Don't give associates an excuse to argue that they did not hear what you said. However, in spite of the need to be forthright, there is no reason to be brutal. Statements like, "That was stupid," are cruel and confrontational and will elicit a strong reaction. Saying, "You have failed," may be truthful, but it may also be so devastating that the associate may simply not listen. Try statements like, "I think you have some areas that could be improved." This approach shows you believe the associate can fix the problem and the short-term failure can be overcome. It provides hope that the feedback will constructively improve the performance. Your goal should be to clearly and directly communicate the constructive evaluation, but you must continue to take all actions based on love.

Andy Grove, in *High Output Management*, offers sound advice about delivering the assessment. "There are three Ls to keep in mind when delivering a review: Level, Listen, and Leave yourself out."[34] By "level" he means to be honest; by "listen" he means just that. "Leave yourself out" means try to avoid the bias of your own thinking.

People Believe What They See: Write Objectively

Another way to deal with your associates' natural tendency to rationalize their own performance is to use the written word. The written word offers a strong dose of reality. Seldom does anybody fail to get the message from written documentation. That is true for positive evaluations as well as negative ones. This impact, however, is not the only advantage. What you write out is much more likely to communicate the essence of your message because writing helps you to sort through key concepts you want to communicate. In addition, you are much more likely to be careful about what you say if you put it into the written form. As a further benefit, writing may help you to clarify your ideas or perhaps to even change them.

Many of us do not enjoy writing and may be convinced that writing evaluations is a waste of time. Typically, organizations require a written performance appraisal. The document we are discussing may satisfy the organization's expectations, but it is not for the organization. It is for you. It is your guide to helping your associate improve. You will be a better leader if you have the ability to give better evaluations.

Don't Accept the Blame

Giving an associate constructive feedback is only half the responsibility. The evaluation process has one more critical step. You must also commit yourself to influencing the associate's behavior. Of course, you cannot make the changes in behavior and performance; only the associate can do that. Your communications to associates must place the responsibility for the behavior and the performance squarely on their shoulders.

All too often, your associates will look to you to either explain their difficulties or to solve their challenges. At times you may be the cause of the difficulty, but in the vast majority of cases, this retort is simply an expression of frustration. The associate knows the problem exists and puts the problem right back on you anyway. Obviously you must consider carefully any assertion that the problem is your fault, but in most instances, you must not accept the burden. Individuals are, in the final analysis, responsible for their own behavior.

Make Plans to Fix the Problems and Follow Up Consistently

Evaluation is useless if there is no change in behavior or performance, and change takes conscious commitment, effort, and a deliberate plan of action. Planning is not just saying, "I plan to do a better job," or "I plan to be a better person." Planning is deciding what the goals are and how to know if they have been achieved. It takes defining specific actions required to make changes, laying out a timetable for doing them, establishing checkpoints along the way, and creating a mechanism to assess if the actions and results are really on track to accomplish the goals. All of that is hard work, and it requires a real commitment. An associate who has a sincere desire and commitment to improve will continue with the ongoing discipline required to achieve the steps on the journey to success. Without that commitment, most associates will fall well short of their original goals, and you will be having the same evaluation discussion later.

That is where a leader can come in. You must follow up on any evaluation. You cannot make the changes, you cannot enforce the commitment, but you can support it. A leader can take several actions to make certain an associate has a reasonable chance for achieving success.

First, you can offer to help the individual develop a plan. Helping an associate work to set goals is a logical extension of your responsibility to establish expectations. By being involved in this process, you are clarifying and enhancing your role as leader. Further, if an associate has not been able to establish a format for the plan, you can help create a structure that works. After it is completed, offer to provide feedback on the plan.

One of the many values of being a part of the self-improvement-plan process is that it gives a leader the opportunity to validate the evaluation feedback's effectiveness. If the plan truly addresses the issues raised in the evaluation, then, at a minimum, you can say you have succeeded in communicating the need for improvement. If the plan does not, then you have an opportunity to refine the process before the associate wastes weeks or months of effort focusing on the wrong issues. This is hard work and requires a leader who feels the sense of love and commitment to the improvement of all associates as they search for their potential achievement level and fulfillment.

BEFORE YOU EVALUATE, PREPARE

- Choose the one person in your unit who needs a counseling session most and prepare an outline of the discussion you will have with that person.
- Describe what you plan to do in order to deal with the most unsatisfactory performer in your unit. Create an action plan for dealing with that person. Be specific about what your expectation is for the result of your plan.
- Practice the session. Role-play with yourself; build your confidence.
- Just to be prepared, assume the session above was not successful. Now prepare a brief on a final session where you will terminate that person.

Second, you can ask associates how they are doing on their personal improvement plan. Simple though that question may be, it can have a profound effect. When the leader asks a question, the staff listens. When the leader listens to the answer and responds appropriately, the staff has been affected. Leaders should never underestimate the influence they have. You are the single most important person in the daily work life of the associate. Your interest in them and your questions to them are powerful.

Third, you can influence an associate by acknowledging improvement. We will look more closely in the next chapter at the power of this act, but suffice to say when you recognize improvement, you have reinforced the behavior.

Evaluation: Evaluate Yourself

If you are getting little constructive evaluation or feedback on your performance, what alternatives do you have? You cannot develop yourself if you have no idea how you need to improve. Evaluation is intended to offer that insight to your associates and, in this case, to you. How often have you received a performance review that really had an impact on you? Probably very seldom.

Try Your Boss First

Consider simply asking your boss for feedback. One bad result that could happen is that she will say no. More likely she will dodge and weave but ultimately give you at least some type of evaluation. You may not like what you hear, but that is what you need to know. If you do get some troubling news, then you will have some advanced warning your job may be at risk. This is a real possibility that happens every day in the world of work. Your goal should be to avoid the ultimate surprise of being terminated for failure when you thought that you were doing a great job. Find a way to get feedback that can help you improve since it might also save your job.

A more likely scenario for your attempt to get an evaluation from a reluctant boss is for you to hear, "Oh, everything is great. Just keep up the great work!" This is actually your worst-case scenario because in all likelihood it is simply not the truth. The comments may be well intended, but they are not enough. You need to receive constructive criticism or compliments that will help you improve. The "everything is great" answer only makes you feel good about everything, and that means not one positive behavior was reinforced and not one negative behavior was corrected. In short, you got nothing but a comment that made you and your boss feel good about her failure to communicate. Keep trying, but this boss is unlikely to give you much more.

Most bosses who are reluctant to give feedback are eventually forced by the organization to do something, but if that process fails, then try writing your own appraisal. How to do that is another question. A good place to start is the performance review forms your organization already uses. Fill out a formal review of yourself using that form. Put yourself in your boss's shoes. Write the review based on what you think her perceptions are, not what you believe to be truth. Most of us know others have different perceptions than we have, and we are usually convinced those perceptions are in error. They are not. Like it or not, your boss's perception is reality for her. Your view is reality for you, but it is irrelevant. When she talks to you, when she talks to others, when she thinks about your performance or potential, she will base those conclusions and comments on her perceptions, not yours.

Perception is important because we all work in a world based on what others believe about us. If their perceptions are different from our view of the truth, then either we are wrong or their perception is wrong. In either case, the disparity between the two must be eliminated. Either we must change their view of us, or we must change our own self-view. Usually you will benefit more from accepting the boss's perception and attempting to correct or improve your performance.

Self-evaluation is tough to do and takes some practice to get it right. The irony is once you take it seriously, you will be more critical of your performance than others might be. Once you begin, this process will be very therapeutic. Start now, and put in motion the forces for improvement. Your best improvement will come from responding to your most significant challenge.

How will you know what you should focus on first or most? The answer is to focus on the observation that is the hardest to accept, the one you are least able to look at objectively. If it truly is the most painful, then it is probably the most significant, deep-seated issue. Starting there can make the largest difference.

Have Others Who Love You Give You Feedback

Once you have given yourself a thorough look, you should then begin the painful process of asking others around you for feedback. If your organization has a 360-degree system, that will help, but what you really want is for peers and subordinates alike to feel comfortable enough with you to tell you what they perceive as your strengths and weaknesses. However, you must be ready for almost any comments. Some will tell you only, "You're great." Others will tell you only what they know you want to hear. Still others will hint in some small way about a weakness, saying it is really nothing significant. Some will flatten you with criticism. Try to be calm and receptive. Of course, if one of your weaknesses is that you cannot accept criticism, then that will be very difficult.

Feedback from associates and peers can have as much, if not more, significance than your boss's feedback. If you are doing a good job in your current assignment, you are likely to get positive feedback from your boss. If, however, you are doing a great job at the expense of your relationships with peers or associates, you might be creating an environment where your current boss thinks you are great and everybody else in the organization is unhappy with you.

Keep in mind, you must carefully choose which colleagues from whom to request feedback. Getting a friend to tell you what you want to hear may feed your ego, but it will not help you focus on those areas you should be addressing. Also, asking people who do not know your boss's expectations, no matter how objective they might be, may lead you to erroneous conclusions, no matter how sincere the feedback.

Focus on Your Weaknesses

Every self-help book advises you to be a positive thinker. It's true; we need to always feel good about ourselves. The fact is, however, our self-concept can be great, and we can be ineffective. I recall one leader with enormously positive self-esteem who achieved significant stature in his organization. The problem: he saw no faults in himself and only weaknesses in the people around him. He trusted no one and loved no one. Worse still, nobody could get close enough to him to tell him what he needed to hear. Eventually, both he and the company failed. To this day, he denies he failed, pointing rather to circumstances that he insists caused the failure. But he did fail. His ability to lead was impaired by his inability to love his associates and be realistic about himself.

Keep your positive self-esteem, but recognize that *everybody* can improve. Recognize your strengths and be certain you continue to behave in ways that maximize the impact of those strengths on yourself and your associates. However, focus also on those areas where you need improvement. This is positive, not negative, thinking. Your thought process must be, "I am good today, and I am going to be better tomorrow. I am positive that I will improve!"

Make the Improvement Plan a Priority

Thinking you will improve and actually improving are quite different. Positive thinking must be turned into positive action. You must be energized to accomplish something. Without a plan of action and the resolve to act, you will achieve no predictable change and certainly will have no way of knowing if you are on course.

But what is a self-improvement plan? Where do you start, and what does it look like? It starts with a decision to seek to understand the areas of your life, be they character traits, leadership skills, or otherwise, that require attention. That means you must use an evaluation mechanism in which you have confidence. The evaluation may have come from a boss, from a peer or friend, or from within yourself. Whatever the case, you must believe that these areas really need your attention, and you must decide you will set goals to address the weakness.

If you accept the conclusion that you have a weakness in financial analysis, for example, then you must set goals that will help you to develop the technical skills required to improve in that area. If that means taking courses, then you need to set a firm date when you will start the course. If you need help with the communication skills required to be an effective coach, then you need to determine the best way to get those skills. It may mean attending a seminar, or it may require reading a few books and then following a disciplined practice program that gives you either role-playing experience with a friend or real work situations in which to use your newfound skills.

Whatever the case, you must establish a need, set a goal, set a specific strategy to achieve the new skills, and then set a date by which you will achieve the developmental experience required to improve your performance. Most important, write all of this down so you can see the plan in real terms. People tend to remember information that impacts multiple senses. Seeing your goals in writing adds to your intellectual and emotional commitment to the plan.

No plan is worth the paper it is written on if all you do is put it in a file and leave it for another day. The plan belongs in your daily planner. It should be a to-do list item every day. It must influence your priorities in the same way that getting the work out affects every day at the job. If you do not treat your own development with the same priority you give to your job, then you will always be a second-class citizen in your world. At a minimum, you must make your own development equally as important as that of your associates. Therefore, you must have a follow-up program that keeps the discipline of improvement at the forefront of your attention.

Every plan element must have a completion date, but just as important, each must also have intermediate checkpoints that provide you with frequent insight into how you are progressing. These progress checks are essential largely because without them the crush of day-to-day priorities will limit your improvement efforts. You have to resist that crush if you want to achieve your goal. At a minimum, every week you should check your performance against your plan. If you are falling behind, you should not wait for six months to go by to decide you have failed to keep the commitment.

Case Study

Cathy is the manager of a small team of analysts who are focused on process improvement in their division. She reports to the division president, Jason, but spends most of her time working with managers who do not report to him. These managers are a couple of levels below the president. The managers report to their supervisors who then report to the president. Cathy's team is responsible for facilitating process improvement projects that effectively improve quality and reduce costs.

Cathy has been in her job for about two years, and today was the first time that the president had actually given her a performance review. Jason had set the appointment about three weeks ago, and this morning Cathy met with him for about forty minutes. Her performance appraisal was actually excellent, and her boss told her he was very impressed with the cost savings she had reported over the last couple years. He told her he needed even more savings, so she should continue to focus on cutting costs in the division.

During the session, Jason gave her some feedback that had been directly reported to him. Several supervisors said they had received complaints from other managers that Cathy was "no fun to work with." He told her she needed to deal with these concerns because they had come from enough different sources to have some validity. Cathy was stunned and took strong exception to the feedback. She told her boss she was going to confront the supervisors to determine who had made the comments, and then go back to those managers and deal with them directly.

Jason responded very strongly that such action would not be acceptable to him. Cathy was stunned once again, but realizing how firmly her boss felt about it, she did not pursue it any further and even committed to doing nothing. Despite that commitment, Cathy became more and more upset following the meeting and convinced herself she needed to do something.

What should Cathy do?

This type of scenario in the performance evaluation process is not unusual. Several problems exist here, and each compounds the other. First, it is wrong to wait two years before you give feedback to an associate. Jason is apparently like so many "executives" who simply do not believe they should be required to do formal performance appraisals. If they do conduct formal performance appraisals, it's when they "have the time." Jason's appraisal was weak in many respects, but the manner in which he brought up the feedback on the "fun to work with" allegation was wholly unproductive. What that means is anybody's guess. Had he taken the time to pursue the question with his direct reports, he might have been able to offer meaningful and constructive feedback. Instead, he left it to Cathy to figure it out.

On the receiving end, Cathy did not react well. An emotional retort is not constructive. Her lack of composure prevented her from finding out what the feedback meant because her boss told her to do nothing ... another boss blunder. The end result is the feedback is both disconcerting and useless to everybody concerned, most importantly to Cathy.

So what can Cathy do? Cathy must go back to Jason, after she has cooled off and thought through her response. She needs to ask Jason what the feedback really means, and what he suggests she do to correct it. My guess is Jason has no clue as to what it means. It could mean that she is obnoxious and impossible to work with, or she is so focused on work and achieving her goals she has very little sense of humor. It could mean she is competent but literally no fun. Jason's response would be dramatically different depending on which extreme might be true.

Whatever the case, Cathy and Jason must decide how she should proceed. Cathy cannot continue to be upset, and she should not be prevented from determining what the feedback means. It is Jason's responsibility to clarify the feedback, and it is most critical for Cathy to understand and deal with this perception.

CHAPTER SIX

REWARDS—An Organization Elicits the Behavior It Rewards

At a very early stage in my managerial career, I walked into the office of a new boss and saw a sign on his wall that read, "An organization elicits the behavior it rewards." This man ultimately became my most important mentor, and his message has stayed with me ever since.

To use a simple analogy, a dog behind an invisible fence learns not to go outside the boundary because he gets an electric shock when he crosses it. By the same token, he learns to sit on command when he is given a treat for doing it correctly. In short, there are two ways to learn—one through threat or punishment, one through reward. Although we humans are far more complex than dogs, the same principles of learning can apply to us. The message in this chapter is that if you truly know how to love, then be positive. Although punishment has some value, the value of rewards is far greater. We learn what we should be doing when we are rewarded for the behavior.

As children we learn the word *no* or *not* very early. As we explore the new things we encounter, our parents often try to protect us from mistakes by telling us "no." Leaders need to break what I call the "Cycle of No." Every time you think of the word *no* as an answer or as a statement, try a positive version of that response. Focus on what *to* do, instead of what *not* to do.

TRY THE POSITIVE FIRST

* **Instead of** "No, you may not have the day off."

     Try "I would like you to take next Thursday off instead. Will that work for you?"

* **Instead of** "Do not leave that box in the middle of the room."

     Try "Please put the box in the corner. It will be safer for all of us."

* **Instead of** "I am very unhappy with the quality of your assembly work. You are going to have to stay tonight for another two hours to fix the rework problems."

     Try "Yesterday you had great quality on your production. I would like to compliment you on that and ask you to help me learn why today's production was so problematic by comparison. Maybe we can find the problem so you will not have to stay overtime to rework all the problem pieces"

* **Instead of** "You have been behaving very rudely toward your associates for several months. It must stop. If it does not, you are going to be either transferred or terminated."

     Try "Joe, I was very pleased just then when you spoke nicely to Frank. That is the way I would like you to treat everybody. If you do that, I think that your relationships with the other associates will improve and you will have a chance to be considered for promotion a great deal sooner."

* **Instead of** "Sally, stop doing that. It's the wrong way."

     Try "Sally, here is what I would like you to do. This is going to save you a significant amount of time and energy."

Negative Feedback Creates Fear; Fear Creates Flight

Using rewards to reinforce desired behavior is better than using punishment to eliminate unacceptable behavior. The reason is simple:

punishment can lead to serious negative reactions resulting from a fear of failure. Give adults the opportunity to be rewarded for outstanding performance and they will focus on doing what it takes to achieve the goal. Tell adults they will be fired if they fail to meet a goal and in all likelihood their focus will be on avoiding failure rather than striving for success. Fear can motivate, but it can also paralyze. If we fear something enough, we will spend our time attempting to avoid it. Achieving a goal because of fear will not assure a continued commitment to success. An associate may respond to a negative feedback session with an immediate surge of adrenaline-driven energy, but he may also feel long-term anger that can destroy effective learning and ultimately lead to resentment and resignation.

The emotion of fear at first causes a normal reaction of flight. We fear, we flee. But running from a fear generally gets us nowhere but tired. In some cases, that flight reaction can lead to denial of reality. When we are so afraid that we deny reality, then what we fear cannot happen. If it cannot happen, then we have nothing to fear. Therefore, we are safe.

In our work life, we run from problems in the same way. We pretend they are not really problems; hence, we can ignore them. Even the most well-adjusted people have the ability to ignore problems, hoping they will go away. So when our boss creates a fear that we will lose our jobs if we fail, one option is to assume the boss really does not mean it and ignore the problem.

Another reason people freeze when confronted with fear is because they do not know what to do to succeed. They become immobilized and do nothing, not because they are trying to avoid work, but because they do not know what to do. They are afraid to take any action for fear it will create failure. Signs of this problem range from staring out a window to absence from work for protracted periods.

Another type of reaction to fear can be a physical or mental shutdown. The body gets strong messages from the brain that something is wrong, reacts in a psychosomatic way, and becomes ill.

The medical community has become acutely aware of the mind–body connection. The field of holistic medicine has emerged in recognition of the idea that emotional events such as intense fear can trigger very serious illnesses. These illnesses are not just in the mind. They are real, physical illnesses that can destroy a person. These reactions can range all the way from stress headaches to heart attacks, from rashes to severe immune system deficiencies.

In short, fear does work to push people, but leading by fear can have negative psychological and physiological impacts on associates. Why would a person who loves others create that type of "dis-ease"? Although punishment is sometimes necessary, it must be used sparingly and only when rewards fail to deliver results. Unfortunately, punishment frequently fails with people who have not responded to rewards, either.

At times punishment is the only option, but it always carries the risk of adverse reactions. When somebody makes a serious error, the first action may be negative feedback. As an example, if a machine operator endangers a coworker's life or a clerk's error could have resulted in a $1 million loss, negative feedback is obviously required, even though there is a reasonable risk of serious adverse consequences from the associate's reaction. No reasonable leader could be expected to hold back from the emotional reaction of a first-class scolding. The key to managing this negative feedback is to follow up with constructive corrective action. Turning a negative into a positive is a must if you want to provide a real developmental experience.

Sometimes You Have No Choice but to Be Negative

Every leader has abandoned "rewards only" leadership more than once. At times, the only possible action is a negative action. It is natural to expect you will get a negative reaction in return, so make certain the advantages outweigh the impact of that negative reaction. Fear and anger, the natural reactions in response to criticism, can energize or enervate. Assess the potential result of an associate's unfavorable reaction to your negative feedback and decide if you can live with the consequences. As I said earlier, negative feedback probably is best reserved for times when you have had no real success with other attempts.

The real issue here is not always related to the situation or to the associate involved. It may also be related to your prior behavior. When a tough boss with a reputation for being critical gives a strong dose of negative feedback, one of two things may happen. It may simply be viewed as just another incident, or it may be viewed as one incident too many. On the other hand, when a normally mild-mannered, quiet, positive leader turns negative, the change will probably be strong and full of surprise and dramatic influence.

Your associates will expect you to be upset when a truly horrible situation develops. Remember, if you do not identify a problem, you cannot help people improve themselves. For this reason, even though you want to focus on positive feedback, it is also essential that your associates understand where their weaknesses are. Negative feedback, or a focus on failure, is inevitably a part of even a positive approach to changing behavior. Do not recoil from identifying weaknesses just because you are trying to focus on the positive. In short, do not let the "be positive" message prevent you from getting the improvement your unit needs.

Rewards Will Reinforce Behavior—Good or Bad

Organizations do elicit the behavior they reward, whether the behavior is good or bad. Contain the negative impacts by making certain your rewards, explicit and implicit, are focused on the behavior you view as good.

Let's consider a few simple examples. Imagine an organization with an incentive system that rewards the sales and marketing departments by paying a flat commission on all sales over $1,000. The range of pricing for the products is $500–$25,000. Let us also assume the profit on a $25,000 item is thirty times greater than the profit on a $1,000 item. Obviously, the company would like the sales force to sell as many large-ticket items as possible since they generate more profits with those items. Although the incentive structure encourages sales over $1,000, we can be fairly certain the staff will not pay much attention to selling items with a higher profit margin since the incentive offers no extra reward to them and $1,000 sales are likely easier. The company encourages sales but not the ones it really wants.

In another case, we can look at a company with an open-door policy for employees. Let's assume employees are told that if they have a problem with their supervisor they always have the right, and indeed are encouraged, to take the issue to the next higher level of management. Many very fine companies have such policies, and they can be quite effective at giving employees meaningful "escape valves" for legitimate supervisory problems.

In this example, the company has had this policy for three years, and it seems to be working to everybody's satisfaction, except in one department. In this department, several supervisors have complained to the human resources department about the policy, saying it substantially undercuts their ability to manage. The director of human resources is concerned and conducts an investigation. He finds there are ten times as many complaints in that department.

On further investigation, he discovers that when the department manager receives a complaint, he always overrules the supervisor. In other words, the complaint is always resolved in the employee's favor.

It is possible every supervisor in that department has a leadership problem; however, it is more likely the manager has created the problem because he rewards each complaining employee by always agreeing with the complaint. Over time, employees in his department have realized that if they complain, they get their way; therefore, they should always complain.

As you can tell in each of these examples, it does not take long for associates to "break the code." In the first instance, they figure out how to make the most money, and they use the easiest way to do that. In the second instance, they conclude they can have anything they want just by filing a complaint up the chain of command. The organizations elicited the behavior they rewarded. The only problem was it was undesired behavior.

Ironically, the second example is the most frequent mistake leaders make. In the first instance, most organizations put serious thought into such an incentive plan, and it will, in all likelihood, be adjusted to encourage high-profit sales long before it is implemented. In the second instance, the policy probably has safeguards built in, but its execution is a leadership responsibility. The manager is rewarding undesired behavior in spite of a sound policy.

Leaders do this very often without recognizing the impact. We do it when we allow an unsatisfactory employee to continue in a job long past the time we should have taken adverse action. We do it when we promote the wrong person. We do it when we allow a person to come in late almost every day without any disciplinary action. In each of these circumstances, we reward the wrong behavior by allowing it to continue. All associates get the message, and they will begin to exhibit the undesired behavior. Like it or not, all of our decisions are on stage.

For example, if your associates see promotions based on personal charisma of people whom they know to be lazy, they will conclude that the way to success is to be a nice person who goes home early. Much sooner than you might expect, you will see your entire staff race to the door at 4:30 p.m. every day.

It is important to give rewards for the right behavior with the right associates. Norm Augustine, author of the classic book *Augustine's Laws*, tells it this way: "Recognition of accomplishment (and the lack thereof) is an essential form of feedback. To reward poor performance or neglect outstanding performance is like placing the controls for each separate half of an electric blanket on the wrong side of the bed. Think about it."[35] If you do, it will be clear that such a leader is sending all the wrong signals to all the associates.

WATCH OUT FOR
MISLEADING REWARDS

Here are a couple examples of how the correct intent can lead to the wrong result.

The intent: To motivate an associate to increase throughput at the workstation by providing an incentive to speed up production.

The tactic: Tell an associate he can go home just as soon as he finishes the assembly of the last twenty units on his workstation.

The result: The associate speeds up the process and completes the units and leaves one hour early. The units have a defect rate that is three times the associate's normal rate and five times that of the unit as a whole.

The intent: To improve a weak associate's performance by offering an added incentive to meet the quality standards of the unit.

The tactic: Tell the worst performing associate if he achieves the customer service satisfaction standards he will get a day off of his choosing.

The result: The associate achieves the improvement in performance and is rewarded with a day off. The best performing associate finds out about the reward and is incensed and insulted because he needs a day off to take an ailing child for medical tests but he has no more days off. He starts looking for another job because he thinks the company does not appreciate his work.

Cash Always Has a Benefit, but Less Than You May Realize

Financial rewards are positive behavior reinforcements. In fact, most leaders consider cash to be king. Every survey ever done by researchers has financial rewards as a useful factor, but virtually no surveys provide conclusive evidence that financial rewards are the most important. When you look to reward associates, you will always have financial rewards in your quiver, but it cannot be the only arrow. That said, never ignore financial rewards. They matter, and they should be used when appropriate.

WHEN USING FINANCIAL REWARDS, USE THESE QUESTIONS TO DECIDE WHAT TO DO

- Think about the last salary review you completed and the conversation you had with your staff member. Was the salary increase a good increase by your standards? If so, did your staff member appreciate it? Did the salary increase actually reward performance? Did it encourage that person to do even better? Has that person done better since the increase was given?

- Does your organization have an incentive system that rewards top performers? How does it operate, and how do you apply it to your staff? Has it worked to recognize performance? Has it worked to encourage performance?

- Make a list of the top five financial rewards you plan to use during the next six months to reward performance.

- Do you believe the associate whose performance you are going to reward is "money motivated"? How can you make that decision? What happened when you last gave that associate a merit raise? Have you ever used a financial or cash reward to reinforce behavior in that associate? How did it work?

Catch Them Doing Something Right

When you housebreak a pet, the training key is to reward, or punish, behavior quickly. In the same way, you must catch your associates doing something right and reward them for it quickly. They, too, will remember the correct action a great deal better if the reward is on the spot, rather than substantially delayed. The same goes for errors. It makes no sense to give an admonishment six months later. Do it immediately.

PLAN FOR THE RIGHT REWARDS

- What is your plan to catch the correct behavior?
- Have you trained your associates to know what the right behavior is?
- Make a list of five non-financial rewards you will use to reward performance on the spot when you catch somebody doing something right.
- Make a list of each person in your unit. Beside the names indicate what is most important to that person. On that same list, identify something you could do for or give to each individual as a reward for accomplishing a specific goal. Also list one thing you think you could hold out to them to receive as an incentive reward for reaching a goal.
- Describe the one reward you have received that was the most powerful incentive for you to continue to perform at an exceptional level. Would it apply to anybody in your unit?
- Create a list of those programs you would like to see your organization create so you can use them to motivate or reward your staff. Make certain at least half are programs that would involve little or no money. Now rank the list in order of your most desired.
- Write a detailed plan for getting your organization to implement one of the programs you listed.

In the United States, we are not a society focused on patiently waiting for long-term feedback. We tend to want our feedback immediately, not later. When we look for rewards, the same is true. Given this reality, we, as leaders, need to look for ways to reward positive behavior and results. Look for small rewards, as well as large ones. If a person you have coached on interpersonal skills comes to the office with a particularly pleasant demeanor and takes the time to be nice to a colleague, then you should take the time to reward that behavior, right then and there. If a sloppy worker does a particularly good job of cleaning up his workstation, reward him immediately. If a secretary you have coached about a lack of persistence finds a document she has been searching for days to find, give her a reward right then. If a salesperson closes a sale he needed in order to make his goal for the month, reward him. In every respect, catch your associates doing something right and reward them for it immediately. You will be amazed at the impact.

Use Praise, Not Just Money

How should you reward your associates? Remember that recognition is far more powerful than monetary rewards. Of course, it is important to pay people what they are worth, and often what they are worth changes as their performance improves. Compensation is not irrelevant, yet it has much less of an impact than most leaders expect. People will do almost the impossible if they think they are appreciated and if they are being led by a person who cares (loves).

Praise can be an art form, or it can be a waste of time. When associates do the right thing or get the right result, they must know the leader noticed. But noticing is not enough. Be certain you communicate your approval of their performance and that you want them to continue to achieve that same success in the future. The real issue for a leader is to know when and how to reward.

Again, make certain you pick the right time to reward. You should always find a way to reward for success when expectations are achieved. It is particularly important to reward those efforts that result in successes where failure existed before or when a major milestone has been achieved along an improvement plan. Always try to make the reward or praise happen right after the success.

GIVING REWARDS
IS ALMOST AN ART FORM

Cash rewards usually are effective rewards, but you will always be amazed at how effective non-cash rewards can be. Give an associate something that can be symbolic of a success and can be seen and admired by others and you will almost always enhance the associate's self-esteem. Try some of these suggestions of how and when to give rewards:

* A praising comment
* Flowers
* Candy
* A trip to Hawaii
* A note saying "Thank you"
* A phone call saying "Good work"
* Public approval
* Comments in a meeting about an achievement
* An e-mail containing praise, with a copy to the HR file
* A party in the person's honor
* A pizza party for the entire unit
* Lunch
* A cup of coffee at break time
* A visit to the person's desk to tell him he did a "great job"
* A formal letter to the file noting extraordinary performance
* A handshake
* Some marketing material with the company logo (e.g., pen, letter opener, sweater, tie)
* Golf balls for a golfer
* A formal, rotating trophy for "Associate of the Month"
* A certificate of appreciation framed for the wall in the person's workspace
* A $100 on-the-spot bonus for something extraordinary
* An item from the organization's formal recognition program

Rewards: Reward Your Own Success

So far, leading yourself has been hard work. Your natural reaction will be to say, "All this work deserves a reward." You must resist rewarding hard work. Never allow yourself to fall into the trap of confusing efforts with results. An improvement plan is great, and you should feel good about getting to that stage, but feeling good is not enough. Reward yourself only when you achieve a goal.

The whole concept of self-reward assumes you know how to deny yourself what you want. Perhaps the most significant difficulty in applying your LEADERSHIP strategy to yourself is the issue of discipline. When you apply these concepts to your associates, you are the person in power. You control the leadership efforts, and you also control the final reward. You can give rewards when you think they are deserved, and you can deny them when you believe an associate has fallen short. Rewarding yourself, on the other hand, requires you to play two roles—the "rewarder" and the "rewardee." This requires significant personal discipline. You must deny yourself a reward until you have a real achievement. If a reward is truly something you want, it will take great will and commitment to avoid cheating. If you resist, the reward will have a twofold benefit. First, you will reward the improvement in behavior you have been targeting. Second, you will reinforce personal discipline, which is itself a major behavioral characteristic that will pay huge dividends throughout your career and life. What a bargain: two lessons in one.

Be certain to keep the rewards in perspective; save the big rewards for big accomplishments. A trip to Hawaii should be saved for a major milestone (like completing a full degree program, not just finishing a single course). This point may seem obvious, but it is easy to fall into this trap. What will you do for the really big accomplishment if the small ones get huge rewards? Unless you inherited a multimillion-dollar fortune, you will quickly run out of carrots and have only the discipline stick to keep you focused on big improvements.

You will find that the joy of achievement can itself become a powerful reward. In addition, you will become conditioned to continuous improvement as a way of life, rather than as an event you must force-feed yourself. This will happen in large part because you will continue to see improvement in your life and your career as you follow your development plan.

The other side of this process is punishment. You will generally have an easier time developing punishment systems for your associates than you will for yourself. This is because of the discipline factor. How do you punish yourself? Does punishment mean giving yourself pain, or does it mean denial of something you want?

You may feel a need to punish yourself when you fail, but you must focus on what you will do to avoid the next mistake or failure in the future, not on the failure itself. Even if you can create a punishment that hurts you enough to motivate you to anger, getting angry has value only if it motivates you to take action to rectify the cause of the failure. Anger that is not directed toward constructive action often turns into remorse, regret, or self-pity. None of these will contribute to your achievement of a goal.

Regret is a useless burden. Mistakes are to be learned from. Learn to forgive yourself and to use your mistakes as stories that will help others years from now. Use the mistake today as a basis for forming a new goal and a new plan to achieve your intended improvement, and make certain you avoid making the same mistake once again.

The only effective way to follow up on a success is with a reward; the only effective way to follow up on a failure is to set a new goal and achieve it. Punishing yourself does not work any better than punishing your associates.

Case Study

"Laura, I need to talk to you!"

Laura had heard these words from her boss before. They always gave her a headache. "Here we go again," she thought, "another tongue-lashing."

Before Laura could see what Betty wanted, the phone rang. She had been waiting for a callback from an irate customer and wanted to take the call. But given her boss's tone of voice, she decided to go see her first.

Betty noticed Laura ignoring the call, and before Laura could say anything, she said, "You know how we all are trying to improve our customer service rankings. Letting that call go unanswered is clearly not great customer service. And that is what I want to talk to you about. I got another complaint call about you; this time on your phone etiquette. Laura, I cannot understand how this happens. I have talked to you about this problem several times in the past year, and you do not seem to get the message. The last time I put you on probation and gave you a thirty-day warning. That seemed to get your attention. But within another six months, you did it again. I am getting fed up with your inability to learn. What do you have to say for yourself?"

By now, Laura was beginning to have another one of those spells her therapist called an anxiety attack. She was starting to feel weak; her breathing was becoming rapid; and she knew soon she would start hyperventilating. The fear was getting so severe she felt she was going to pass out.

Her boss looked at her and said, "What is wrong with you? You look awful."

Laura could barely catch her breath long enough to say, "I am having an attack. The doctors warned me about them. Please help!"

Betty tried to calm her, but she kept getting whiter and whiter. Panicked, Betty started shouting at people in the office to call 911. Fortunately, one of the associates, Carol, knew how to handle hyperventilation. Carol rushed to her desk, dumped her lunch out of a paper bag, and put it over Laura's mouth. After a few minutes, Laura began breathing more normally. The crisis seemed to have passed.

Betty turned away and went back to her office. A couple of hours later, she came by and asked Laura how she was. "Oh, by the way, I got two letters complimenting you on your customer service today. I thought you might want them. I hope you feel better tomorrow."

Who needs a performance improvement: Laura, Betty, or both?

If Laura's performance is consistently below Betty's standards, then she definitely needs to improve. It is hard to say based on one complaint in the last six months and two letters of praise whether Laura's performance truly is lacking or if Betty is simply being hard on her. From the tension that

Laura feels whenever her boss calls her name, it can be inferred that Betty criticizes her on a regular basis.

Furthermore, Betty's attitude when reprimanding Laura about the complaint was aggressive and unsympathetic. It seems that Betty is more of a tyrant than a leader. In many respects, Betty's performance as a leader needs improvement.

Betty may have good reasons to be disappointed in Laura. If that is the case, she should have helped her improve through development, coaching, and effective use of rewards for improvement. Periodically scolding her for bad behavior is not a constructive way to elicit positive changes. The two letters of praise that Betty gave Laura at the end of the day would have been a perfect opportunity to reward her for performing well. Instead, Betty handed them over shortly after criticizing her, and she did so without offering much praise of her own. Rewards are an essential part of leadership, and Betty needs to learn to use them effectively if she hopes to have loyal, successful performers on her staff.

CHAPTER SEVEN

SYSTEMS—Structure Frees the Mind to Be Creative

In all the previous chapters, the focus has been primarily on activities the leader executes and how they directly impact staff behaviors and, ultimately, the unit's performance. In this chapter, the focus is on the unit, how it performs its role, and, most important, what the leader must do to structure the activities of the unit as a whole. The word *systems* is used to describe all of the structure the leader establishes to assure the unit achieves peak performance.

In the field of biology, scientists refer to "ecosystems" to describe the connected workings of the environment and the interactions of the organisms living within that environment; in information technology, analysts refer to the program systems that control a computer; in medicine, doctors refer to the body's various groupings, such as the nervous system, the digestive system, etc., where these systems define how the body handles the complex functions of life. In all of these, the common element is this: a variety of activities are coordinated in some way to accomplish a functional objective.

In organizational leadership, systems are those structures that support the leader and provide assurance that the staff and other resources deployed to achieve organizational results are coordinated in a way that accomplishes the desired results. Without these systems, or processes, the workplace would be in chaos. The organization's structure and processes support effective leadership in the achievement of peak performance. These "systems" are an essential principle for the effective leader, and the effective leader must be capable of coupling behavioral skills with process disciplines in order to achieve peak performance. Further, these systems must be built with a keen sense of the role that love plays in leading. The loving leader cannot allow the systems to dehumanize the associates. We as leaders must always remember that these are humans we are leading, not machines.

In the very early days of Frederick Taylor and the emergence of "scientific management," it was clear that most managers were attempting to create a workplace where the humans working there were trained and managed to replicate all tasks in a very mechanical and routine way. Even today, the average worker is expected to do repetitive tasks in a manner that replicates the best practice. When we as leaders focus on the concept of replication and repetition, we must never forget that our staff leaves to live life as a member of society, that a staff member does not get turned off at the end of a day as if a machine.

Systems Support Leadership

It is important to keep the systems principle in the proper perspective. Systems support the previously discussed core principles. Systems cannot stand alone, nor can they take precedence over the leadership activities discussed throughout this book. Systems are a necessary condition for success, but they are not a sufficient condition. Love must never get lost as we create these systems.

There was a time when the academic and business communities became so enamored with systems and quantitative methods that the role of human behavior in the leadership function was dramatically deemphasized. This intellectual blunder led to a generation of people in charge who thought intellectual and analytical capability was all that was needed to succeed. That generation, many of whom are in senior executive positions today, changed the culture of the organizations they led. Many of the illnesses in organizations today can be linked to their perspectives. Much of the employee disaffection in the recent past can be attributed to the failure of organizational leadership to understand and appreciate the necessity of leading employees (with love) as well as managing systems.

The role of all systems (process or structure) is to support leaders and staff by freeing their minds to accomplish the most creative activities while assuring goals are achieved. Great leaders use systems leadership but are not slaves to those systems. As the chapter title says, these systems should be used to free a leader's creativity and allow them time to be the loving leaders we have now established they must be to help their team achieve peak performance.

If a system becomes the leader's primary goal or focus, the organization's priorities are likely to be lost in trivia. The "Law of Administrivia," which was discussed earlier, describes how excessive focus on systems creates dysfunctional behavior. One of the great thinkers on the role of systems and process in organizations was Edwards Deming. He believed process was the only thing that could be managed in order to control results. It is probably true that process is the only thing that can be managed, but no one who is "in charge" can accomplish organizational goals by merely focusing on the process. While systems, or processes, support managerial functions required to achieve measurable results, a commitment to human behavior is the key to effectively leading associates in the pursuit of those results.

In some environments, electro-mechanical devices that perform some, or all, of the manual component of human labor are doing most of the work. Managing those machines is literally "mechanical," but generally there are humans maintaining those machines; programmers program them, schedulers allocate the workload, etc. In each of these cases, mechanical systems are used to support the human energies that create the factory's output. Processes must be put in place, but they must be thought of as helpful to the leader and staff, not the primary focus of leadership.

It is possible, indeed probable, for a manager to manage the machines we use as part of the production process without ever knowing how to love, but that is not true about the human resource. Leaders must create systems that facilitate success *for* the humans, not create an environment in which the humans are treated like machines. Our organization must always be seen as an organization of humans who are connected to the mechanical and electronics aids with the sole purpose of creating value to other human beings. If we lose that human connection, then we can never be an effective leader; we will simply be an "overseer."

The Hemispheres of the Brain

Few readers of popular or professional literature have escaped reading about the differences that exist in the physiology, and apparent functioning, of the brain's hemispheres. Most of us, at one time or another, have been asked to define our own thought patterns as either "left brain" or "right brain" thinking.

This model of brain functions is used to explain, or stereotype, the behavior patterns of individuals. With the manifestation of a logical thought process, the label of "left brain" is attached. Show a creative effort and the label becomes "right brain." The scientific study of these stereotypes is sufficiently credible to assume that the labels frequently are reasonable approximations of the dominant personality, but seldom does a simple label define the whole personality.

As an example of these stereotypes, each of the six previous LEADERSHIP principles probably would be viewed with either a right- or left-brain bias. When the leader practices love, she will be right-brained; when she sets expectations or makes assignments, she will be left-brained; when she focuses on development, she will probably be labeled a right-brained leader; when evaluating, the label is likely to be left-brained; when rewarding, right-brained. Obviously, interpreting each of these behaviors in such a binary manner would be naïve. Although many believe people have a dominant or "more prevalent" inclination, it is probably much more reasonable to use the model as a way to differentiate between types of behavior, rather than to generalize a dominant pattern for the totality of a leader's behavior.

One thing should be clear; it is very easy to believe that the right brain is responsible for the love thinking and behavior. Logic is probably not the essence of our ability to love. It may be logical to love, but it is probably not logical that we actually love. Hence, love may be found "in the right brain"; it is clearly recognized by the left brain as the logical action to achieve success as a leader.

From these simplistic observations, it is clear the emotional and creative aspect of the brain function is critically active during many leadership activities; although, there are certain aspects of leadership that require a strong focus on the more "scientific" aspects of thinking. The deployment of the "systems" principle is clearly one such aspect. While systems are the structure that assures organizational execution, system design can benefit greatly from a clear understanding of a related discipline called "systems thinking."

Systems Thinking—The Obvious That Is Often Ignored

The principles of systems thinking entered the popular world of leadership reading through a groundbreaking work, *The Fifth Discipline*, written by Peter Senge. In his book, he walks the reader through the core principles of this rather elegant description of decision-making processes and structure. The essence of systems thinking is not simply that logical thinking is important, but that in trying to evaluate issues, solve problems, or create alternative futures, we must see the world through the lens of interrelatedness and interdependence. The process of systems thinking demands that we always look at the whole process, all the relevant variables, and how they interrelate to each other in causing the current state. Every action we take has a consequence, and every consequence causes another action. These observations define a world that is not linear, but rather is a series of action loops that either dampen or reinforce the original action.

Here is one of the simplest examples of how systems in the real world behave in ways we may not predict with linear world thinking: adjusting the water temperature in a shower. When we first turn on the shower, the water is relatively cold because most of the water that comes out first was sitting in the pipes, unheated. If we turn on the hot and cold water at the same time, the first flow will be cool to lukewarm. If we turn the hot water up to full capacity to increase the temperature, eventually the hot water will dramatically increase the temperature of the water flow and the water will be too hot. Hence, we will turn up the cold water to cool down the flow again. However, there is always a delay in the adjustment's impact on the flow, and we must compensate for that delay in order to gauge our next move. Unless we stop and think about what is happening, we could spend a rather long time reacting with water flow changes that never get a chance to fully adjust before we are making another adjustment.

Usually we break the "system code." Once we realize what is happening, we can then wait for the time of the delay and determine the net impact of our last adjustment. When we do that, the time it takes us to end up with a comfortable water temperature is dramatically reduced. Our adjustment of behavior is the result of systems thinking. We realize that the system has a delay and that we must look at the entire system to get the desired result.

Such thinking is essential for the leader to consider. When we are dealing with human behavior as leaders, we are dealing with complex systems, and we must know and understand that taking one action will not always have a simple, linear result. One action can precipitate a reaction from our associates, which then creates a whole new workplace situation. We then are forced to take other actions, or behave in a way that reacts to the new situation. In a theoretically linear world, A may cause B, and then B may cause C. But in real life, often there is a next step where C then impacts or "causes" A. This looping is now reinforcing the original action, so that once you have put the sequence in place, the results will reinforce the first action and intensify the result, maybe even to the point of "unacceptable results."

An example of this might be (A) a serious counseling session with your associate indicating she is being too critical of her peers, which then causes your associate to respond immediately by (B) dramatically reducing her communications with her fellow workers. This action (B) then causes her fellow workers to continue the mistakes the so-called "critical" worker was catching because now the initiative to give associate feedback has been dramatically reduced. With the reduced communications, the fellow workers sense a withdrawal by the "critical" associate and they dramatically curtail communication, an event we'll label (C). With this series of events, the less feedback the "critical" associate gives, the higher the likelihood she will stop offering feedback to her fellow workers altogether. Overall, the mistakes will actually increase because now the corrective feedback from the "critical" associate is missing.

Over the long run, stopping the feedback would doom the company if there is nobody to pick up the issue. Here is an opposite but similar situation: An employee offers critical feedback. The second associate takes some action to fix the problem. If the first associate continues the high level of negative feedback, then the second associate may continue attempting to resolve the issue but may eventually respond negatively to the ongoing critical feedback. In addition to changes in the process that may temporarily fix the problem, the overreaction could cause increased tension that eventually causes the team to fall apart. The negative feedback strains associate job satisfaction, eventually causing the entire group to become estranged from the process and perhaps even from each other.

The key to remember with systems thinking is that there are virtually no linear, unlinked events in the workplace. Almost all actions, or analyses, will lead you to the connection of a series of actions that eventually loop back to the beginning. Not only does "every action cause an equal and opposite reaction," every action also probably starts five other actions, some of which will come back to the initiator of the initial reaction. Eventually virtually all straight-line processes loop back to the beginning of the process and impact the beginning point.

The lesson is that nothing we do creates one, and only one, reaction. Our behaviors have a multitude of impacts, and we must be sensitive to the possibility that what we do "to or for" our associates will eventually have an impact on us and, in turn, how we act during the next stage of the process. Some might call this a ripple effect, but it is one that has a boomerang effect, often returning to its source.

Another example of this could be the use of love in the workplace. In the event that a leader decides that being a "loving boss" is the right way to lead, then action will be taken to behave in a different (loving) way. That action, although designed to encourage the associate to respond positively to the caring boss, might just cause behavior on her part that ultimately creates a sense of comfort and confidence that she cannot, or will not, be disciplined. This conviction can then lead to an associate becoming irresponsible since she perceives that the boss has concluded not to be "tough." The end result could be that the associate abuses the value of a "loving act" and her performance deteriorates. Obviously, the newfound love by the boss has been implemented in a way, and at a time, that confuses the associates. Unfortunately, this reaction by the associate could cause the boss to conclude that her efforts were wrong, and she might even attempt to counteract this problem with being so tough as to now convince the associate that she is unpredictable and mercurial. Clearly, this is a feedback loop with undesirable and unintended consequences.

Process Management Disciplines

Given that much of the "hard core" leadership work is left brained, many of us search for a compromise that would allow us to be creative and flexible. Leaders in management tend to make one of two assumptions: 1) when they tell one of their employees to do something, that is sufficient; or 2) they need to follow up constantly to assure compliance with the instructions. Both of these can have disastrous impacts. In most cases, leaders who assume compliance are setting themselves up for failure. In the case of the second assumption, the process of constant follow-up is one of those major irritations imposed on a capable staff. Excessive control, or micromanaging, is a fool's burden because once you start that "overkill," you create mistrust with the staff. You also then own all the responsibility for completing the tasks. Your staff will "allow" you to manage the duties, since they then have no bottom-line responsibility for the work. Left-brain thinking is the essential "added principle" that complements the required right-brain behavior of the leader. One way to avoid micromanaging is to have the systems in place to assure you know what the current state of the unit's performance truly is. Together, the leading and the systems give those "in charge" the ability to achieve results.

Enter Peter Drucker

Peter Drucker was probably the greatest thinker and most prolific writer on organizational leadership of the twentieth century. He is often referred to as the father of modern management because more than any other thinker, he spent a large part of his life defining the role of the leader/manager. It is almost impossible to write a book on management without recognizing the monumental reliance we all have on his commitment to making management a "profession" rather than an art form.

Many writers on leadership make such a distinction between leading and managing that they imply the term *management* is a lower order of skill, a position that has no merit. In the world of work, those "in charge" are required to lead and manage. Leading is what we do for, with, and to people; managing is what we do to assure ourselves those goals we are responsible for are actually achieved. Peter Drucker was one of the first to define several critical functions of management that earlier in this book were referred to as the mechanics of management. The critical functions he identified, and those most critical to being an effective leader who implements "systems" to lead, are planning, organizing, directing, and controlling. Remember, these are not a lower order of activity; they are added activities the leader must deploy in order to effectively execute the unit's goals. They are complementary to the first six LEADERSHIP principles discussed earlier.

These functions generally define the activities required to maintain the process disciplines (systems) all leaders must have if the results of their efforts are to be superior and timely. Any leader focused on results must recognize that leading without effective execution by the organization is simply wandering. Effective execution is only possible if the leader has people and processes (systems) in place to generate superior results. As discussed in an earlier chapter, every organizational leader must establish expectations. But simply establishing goals without plans is fruitless. Plans are the pathways that define how we will achieve the results.

The leadership function of "assignment" requires the right people to be assigned to the right jobs. Assignment is a critical first step, but those people must be "organized" and "directed," with organizational structure, effective work processes, and systems to support the plan's execution. In addition to those processes, there needs to be some way to assure the processes are executed properly, and that is the critical role of direction. The leader and his managerial assistants must assure execution occurs. With "direction" in place, the leader and his staff must have the "controls" to make certain that systems are in place to monitor progress and make any mid-course corrections required to achieve peak performance. The leader should delegate many aspects of the plan's execution, but delegation without control is abrogation.

Planning
Setting expectations is the first step in a plan, but plans that make a difference for the leader must be specific and detailed. Accountability needs to be measured both by the assignment of responsibility and a specified time for completion.

Establishing a plan that is vague will likely create a vague result. The need for specificity includes the requirements that were set out in the chapter on expectations. Additionally, the plan must adequately detail the action steps, resources required, assigned responsibility, and deadlines to be met. Timing for completion is a critical element. Plans must be executed in a timely manner or they are not plans, but rather accidents.

Plans must be documented, meaning they must be written. It is not bureaucratic to document a plan; it is necessary. Vague ideas about the plans will create uncertainty and confusion on the part of the staff. An added benefit of writing the plan is there is no better test of clarity in thinking than forcing thoughts onto paper.

Organization

The assignment of staff is essential to execution, but execution will be haphazard at best if the staff and the other resources are not effectively organized to achieve results. Organization can be structured statements (organization charts) of who reports to whom. Organization can also be clear statements of which staff member does which job. It can also be a structure that not only defines who does what but precisely how it is to be done. These structures can be as informal as verbally communicated general guidance to very detailed flow process charts defining each and every step in the process. Regardless of the structure's formality, the details of organization are essential for assigning what to do and how to do it.

Every leader must decide how much and what type of organizational structure is required. Organizations have used the old military model of a pyramid of authority for a very long time. This model continues to be the most common structure to organize the staff. Many other structures have been developed, but few are as simple and straightforward as the "one boss" hierarchical structure. Most organizations use this model, even though shared responsibility through a "matrix" organization has become more popular as organizations grow larger and more complex. In very large organizations, there is a need to coordinate across many different pyramids, and that coordination often requires creating a decision authority to be shared.

The key to success is clarity. The members of your organization must have a clear understanding of their responsibilities and assignments. Any ambiguity regarding these factors will cause confusion and, ultimately, failure to execute effectively.

Directing

No leader should assume issuing instructions will accomplish the goal. There must always be a way for the organization's members to be directed. The traditional model calls for a "boss" who "tells" the staff what to do and engages in activities that assure the staff does the job. Some leaders will do this themselves; in other cases, they will have associates who do it for them.

In the "self-directed" model, the staff or the unit will assume the responsibility to direct their own activities. For many years, management theories have suggested that self-directed teams are even more effective than the "one boss" model. Indeed, it is clear that if the team members are sufficiently motivated and disciplined to self-direct, then that approach will be remarkably effective and efficient, as well as satisfying for the staff. If the team does not come together, or if members do not have the commitment to achieve results, then that process will not be effective.

Whatever model for direction used, there must be some means by which the leader can track the staff's ability to stay focused on the results required. Simply assigning tasks and walking away will eventually lead to inadequate performance.

Controlling

The leader can plan, organize, and direct effectively and still fail. For organizations to achieve the desired results, the leader must have a system of controls in place to monitor the staff's ongoing performance. Even the most automated process requires a mechanism to assure the mechanical processes stay in control. Deming and Joseph Juran changed the course of Japanese (and U.S.) history when they convinced Japanese businesses that the way to achieve success was to institute statistical process controls on the manufacturing processes. These controls assured that when the process was "out of control limits" the leader would know immediately. This knowledge would put the leader in a position to make the appropriate adjustments to assure the output would be within the appropriate tolerances.

The same must apply for every leader's organization. The leader must have process controls. These controls can be as simple as a daily report of the quantity of outputs completed or as complex as a detailed "dashboard" measuring all relevant parameters influencing the results. Whatever the mechanism, the leader must know how the organization is performing, and must know it soon enough to make "mid-course" adjustments. Waiting until the end of the time required to complete a project or achieve a goal is unacceptable. There must be intermediate measures available so the leader knows how the organization is progressing. Without these checkpoints along the way, the probability of success is slim. Once again, delegation without control is abrogation.

Summary

The role of the leader, at any level in an organization, is to energize and focus the staff toward achieving goals. Every leader must have the ability to connect with the staff and to lead them to results. The principles defined in the chapters on expectations, assignment, development, evaluation, and rewards all focus on the people who are being led. In this chapter, we have focused on the systems that are required to support that leadership. Even the best "leader" in the world of work will not be successful in achieving peak performance if he or she does not have the systems in place to assure the success. Leadership is a necessary condition for success; it is not a sufficient condition.

Many leaders of large organizations, including political entities, even countries, frequently forget this and find themselves energizing and developing great strategies, only to find they fail because the energized cannot execute. Great leadership, combined with effective systems and process management principles, enables the leader to deliver on the vision. Without these, the vision, and the passion to achieve, will be an unfulfilled dream.

Systems are intended to make work run more smoothly and efficiently, with less effort and less chance of error. They need to be constantly checked against actual work achievement, as well as updated and maintained to assure they are relevant and current. A calendar that isn't updated with new appointments and deadlines is ineffective as a system of time management; likewise, a database of client and vendor contact information is ineffective if changes and additions are not entered on an ongoing basis. No matter how well an automated system functions, it does not allow an individual to function on autopilot. If autopilot were an option, then a human would not be required to do the job.

USE SYSTEMS RESPONSIBLY

When embraced and used properly, the following systems are simple tools that can help you and your associates achieve success:

Electronic calendars and contact files are time-savers, particularly if they are synched to a personal digital assistant (PDA).

Customer Relationship Management (CRM) software is an efficient way of tracking new leads, client or project status, and follow-up requirements.

A routine management meeting with your staff where the most critical priorities are discussed.

MBWA is the "Management By Wandering Around" acronym Tom Peters made famous. This is itself a system because it allows the leader the opportunity to routinely interface with her staff. This is a "programmed accident."

Each staff feedback session is part of the development system that is so critical to leadership. The systematic focus on helping your associates succeed will be invaluable and will communicate "systems discipline" to them.

Routine management through reporting to your boss gives him the opportunity to know and understand regularly what you are working on and how you are progressing toward the goal. This actually functions as a disciplined system to help you reach your goals by forcing you to report on progress routinely.

Systems: Organize Your Self

Systems provide the structure that allows you to lead a more efficient and productive life. Complicated or complex technology is not required to create an effective system of managing your calendar, your contact file, and your task list. Systems are simply a method of organization that save time and aid productivity. In the era of information overload, we cannot rely on our memories or sticky notes as sufficient reminders to follow through on our tasks. Ironically, this is an age-old problem that was even described by Ben Franklin in his autobiography.

Ben Franklin is typically associated with the Declaration of Independence, bifocals, and the spirit of invention. His name doesn't generally bring to mind "management guru," but an article by Justin Fox, an editor at *Fortune* magazine, offers insightful observations about how this historical figure's life story is full of lessons for modern-day managers. As the owner of a printing shop and publisher of a newspaper, Franklin was a businessman who, like most of us, struggled with time management and order. To combat this problem, he devised a plan to set a daily schedule with goals and tasks assigned in hourly segments of each day. At the end of the day, he asked himself, "What good have I done today?" As Fox astutely observes, Franklin's approach is no different than the best practices that should guide modern management activities.

"This emphasis on setting goals for the day ahead and taking stock afterward remains a staple of time-management advice. (At least, so I'm told.) There's clearly something to it: I know that I'm far more likely to accomplish something when I have a well-defined to-do list for the day. But in a work world where conflicting, competing priorities are the norm, it's really hard to stick to such a list... This is perhaps the most appealing aspect of Franklin's time-management advice: He was an admitted failure at it, and yet that was... okay. Which is just about the most inspirational message conceivable."[36]

Whether or not you succeed in checking each task off of your daily list, you will be more productive and more focused simply by having such a list. This may seem elementary, but it is a system that will help you to set goals and determine which assignments are necessary to achieve your goals. Each assignment should be given a deadline that is reasonable yet ambitious. A sense of urgency is better than the feeling that one has plenty of time to "slack off." At the end of the day, you will have a great sense of satisfaction at how much you were able to accomplish, and be better able to assess what you need to do tomorrow.

ARE SYSTEMS WORKING FOR YOU?

Are systems missing in your routine? To find out, ask these questions. Do you...

* have a drawer full of business cards that have never been entered into a formal contact file?
* have trouble accomplishing both professional and personal tasks on a given day?
* forget to follow through on something because the reminder note got lost in the papers on your desk?
* forget to review your checklist at the end of the day and update it so that you know what you need to do tomorrow?
* feel that there is never enough time in the day?
* spend every weekend doing personal chores that you couldn't fit in during the week?
* spend unnecessary time looking for phone numbers or contact information that you know you should have saved?
* wish you were more organized?

Professional and personal "to-do" lists are critical for us to accomplish our assignments and goals. Whether you need to remind yourself to follow up on a list of client prospects or to pick up the dry cleaning and groceries after work, these are activities that need to be scheduled in your daily plans. In theory, we would all like to keep our professional and personal lives separate, but it is generally a good idea to use the same system for organizing both. It's not practical or efficient to carry two date books or consult two calendars in order to determine your availability when scheduling appointments. Inevitably, that sort of system will result in errors. The most practical solution is to embrace the fabulous, and often free, technology that is available in the form of electronic and online calendars. The same is true for contact information and to-do lists. These systems will truly streamline and simplify your efforts to be organized.

Case Study

Brent was recruited to join a fast-growing Web site development company that provides the whole gamut of services, from designing and building a new site to hosting the site and optimizing it for search engines. Although the company is based in a medium-sized community, it has quickly expanded from servicing local clients to landing some large national accounts. Brent's role as account director means he interacts with clients and also manages the programmers, technicians, and designers who make up the young, creative development team. Before accepting the job, he reviewed many of the Web sites the company had created and was convinced he would be leading a team of highly talented individuals.

After just a short time on the job, it was apparent to Brent he had joined a company in total chaos. For reasons unbeknownst to Brent, a succession of account managers had left the company in the last several months, and the turnover created disorder, confusion, and a lack of accountability. Despite a talented team that put in long hours at work, everyone was far behind on their deadlines. Clients were complaining about the delays and lack of response from the individuals assigned to their Web site projects. The failed deadlines led Brent's boss, Jerome, to put increased pressure on the associates. Rather than acting as a motivating force, Jerome expressed anger and dissatisfaction, which had a negative impact on morale. The work environment reminded Brent of a boiling hot kitchen full of frenzied cooks, none of whom was telling the others what he was adding to the pot on the stove, and none knew what he was supposed to cook. Rather than quit like the many account managers before him, Brent wanted to save his job as well as help his team live up to its potential and achieve success.

Brent analyzed the situation and determined his team would be capable of great work if they were simply given a system that would allow everyone to keep track of project assignments, milestones, and deadlines. He set a meeting with Jerome and presented his suggestion for the company to invest in Customer Relationship Management (CRM) software that would allow him to assign individual workers to each task within a project, control the flow of assignments as each task was completed, and establish deadlines that would be known to everyone involved. With projects so tightly and transparently organized, there would be no confusion as to whether a task had been completed and who was responsible for it.

Jerome liked Brent's idea and commended him for researching the various software options and recommending one that was mid-range in price but had all the capabilities they would need to manage projects. After some discussion, they decided to hire a receptionist who would be responsible for fielding calls and requests from clients and entering those assignments into the system. To prevent the complaint that associates were unresponsive, they would be instructed to forward e-mail requests from clients to the new receptionist, who would also input those assignments into the system. They were further instructed to stay focused by handling their individual tasks according to where they stood in the queue, rather than trying to handle each new task immediately as it came in and thus leaving others unfinished.

Two months after implementing the new CRM system, Jerome called Brent into his office. "Brent, I can't understand what you have done wrong as a manager, but we lost two big clients this week. That's on top of the one we lost last week, and they had been with us since we started the business. As the account director, you are responsible for interacting with clients. You should have known they were unhappy and done something to fix it. We can't afford to lose these clients, and unless you can convince me your team will improve immediately, I don't need to waste any more money on you." Brent was shocked by the client dissatisfaction, and equally shocked by the *caustic attitude of his boss. He understood why Jerome was upset, but Brent didn't feel he was the sole employee responsible for keeping clients happy and on board. Rather than argue the latter point, he decided to get to the bottom of what went wrong.*

"Did the clients explain why they were upset enough to cancel their engagements with us?" Brent asked.

"Yes," Jerome replied, "and it was the same in every case. They said that their requests and problems weren't addressed in a timely manner; their calls and e-mails weren't returned; communication was essentially nonexistent; and deadlines were still not being met."

Brent was once again dumbfounded. "The CRM system should have prevented all of this, and I can't understand what happened because the team is working really long hours," Brent said. He promised to call a meeting of every associate on the development team and get to the bottom of the problem. This was his only hope to solve the problem and save his job.

What went wrong and who is to blame?

What went wrong is the system was left to function on its own without human thought and oversight. Brent should have been monitoring the assignments and their status. He also should have been personally communicating with the clients, as that was a defined part of his job. It is likely the clients' problems were not being assigned a higher priority in the queue, thus leading to the "unresponsiveness" of the team. This could have resulted from the new person not understanding the business and how to determine whether a client's call or request was actually a "burning fire" that needed immediate attention. The individuals on the team were apparently using the system blindly and without attention to whether tasks were being assigned a reasonable priority. They should have been engaged enough to scan the queue and realize a client whose Web site was malfunctioning needed some immediate communication and attention, regardless of whether the receptionist knew enough to put that task at the top of the list.

It seems that everyone in the organization relied on the system to make rational decisions when systems actually work the opposite way: humans have to input information based on rational thought in order for the systems to function as intended. If Brent had communicated with the clients, he would have known they were unhappy; if he had monitored the status of the assignments in the CRM system, he would have known deadlines were not being met.

In regards to blame, Brent has a legitimate reason to be disappointed with his team for failing to communicate with clients and meet deadlines, and in that respect, the team shares responsibility for losing the clients. Brent's boss did not exhibit positive leadership behavior by addressing his staff with anger and abrasive language, and in that sense he, too, shares blame in the situation. However, the bottom line is that Brent is responsible for whether his team is achieving success, and therefore the blame for their failure ultimately rests on his shoulders. The attitude that he is not the only person responsible for the clients' happiness suggests he does not truly understand he has failed as a leader to support his team and give them the human tools (not just automated tools) that are required for success.

CHAPTER EIGHT

HUMOR—Lead with Humble Humor not Hubris

Go ahead and laugh at the irony: humor is a topic that should be taken seriously. Leaders who want the best from their associates must incorporate humor into the workplace. Not to be mistaken for "goofing off" or slapstick jokes, humor is about attitudes and actions that promote health, happiness, teamwork, creativity, and job satisfaction. Organizations that embrace humor employ associates who love coming to work. As a leader, it is your responsibility to lighten up and laugh, and encourage your associates to do the same.

Incorporating humor in the workplace does not mean you should suddenly become a comedian. It is about lightening up the tone, mood, and atmosphere. Diligent, disciplined work is required to achieve the high expectations you set for yourself and your associates. That diligence and discipline needs a counterbalance to promote well-being and alleviate stress. We've all experienced stress and its uncomfortable symptoms such as headache and nausea; however, stress that continues without relief leads to distress, a condition that causes serious adverse health effects. According to a report published by the Cleveland Clinic, "Stress is linked to six of the leading causes of death: heart disease, cancer, lung ailments, accidents, cirrhosis of the liver, and suicide."[37] Studies also indicate stress has a negative impact on the immune system, making those who suffer from stress more prone to illness. The extremely competitive work environment that dominates our society has also increased the level of stress among workers. Furthermore, the need to constantly learn and improve in order to advance is stressful, as is the fear that comes with the potential of losing a job. If too much stress leads to distress and disease, then it is incumbent upon leaders to reduce the stress for themselves and their associates. How? Humor.

The Benefits of Humor

To fully appreciate the many and varied benefits of adding humor into the work environment, one can start with the research that has demonstrated that humor has a significant impact on our health. Studies in publications including the *Journal of Behavioral Medicine* and the *American Journal of Medical Science* support the health benefits of humor. Laughter releases hormones that reduce stress and enhance the immune system; it oxygenates the blood, lowers blood pressure, and relaxes muscles. We all encounter stress on some level in our professional lives, and often this is compounded by stress in our personal lives. Employers who incorporate humor into the workplace will likely have healthier, happier employees. According to Linda Melone PhD, a clinical psychologist and Pepperdine University professor, humor creates positive responses in three ways: "Laughter triggers an emotional uplift. In the work environment, it also triggers our cognitive process and gives us added perspective. Physiologically, laughter counteracts negative thinking and other emotions: chronic anger, anxiety and guilt feelings associated with an increase in the incidence of health problems."[38]

The additional benefits of humor are more abstract but equally appealing for the results it produces. Humor stimulates creativity, positive attitudes, and morale, as well as lessens anger, absenteeism, and turnover. According to humor coach Ann Frey, author of *Laughing Matters*, "A willingness to laugh, plus a sense of lightheartedness, equals a fun, productive workplace. If your employees are happy, they will bring greater energy and enthusiasm to their jobs and your company will function at peak performance. It's not rocket science."[39]

Indeed, humor is not "rocket science," but it is a fundamental joy that is often absent at work. The absence of humor results in employees who are unhappy and inevitably look elsewhere for a job. Employee turnover is expensive to an organization as it takes time and money to interview, train, and integrate each new employee. The current generation of employees expects to work longer hours than were typical for previous generations, but they're also looking for a fun, supportive environment that is more relaxed than the formal, buttoned-up office culture of the past. Studies have also shown that organizations with a fun-at-work ethic are extraordinarily successful. Among the standouts are Southwest Airlines, General Electric, Kodak, AT&T, Money Mailer, Quaker Oats, and Playfair, a company founded by Matt Weinstein, author of *Managing to Have Fun*.

Herb Keller, the CEO of Southwest Airlines, said, "If work is more fun, it feels less like work."[40] Southwest is often used as a case study for a company that encourages humor and fun and can demonstrate that it has a positive effect on the bottom-line results:

- the fewest customer complaints eighteen years in a row, according to the Department of Transportation Air Travel Consumer Report
- profitable for thirty-one consecutive years
- the "Second Most Admired Company," according to *Fortune* magazine
- less than 10 percent employee turnover rate
- a $10,000 investment in the airline in 1972 would be worth more than $10 million today [41]

Why Don't We Use More Humor?

If Southwest and other big-name organizations are using humor and succeeding, why are so many leaders reluctant to do the same? The first reason is perception. They mistakenly believe that humor and laughter in the workplace means associates are not doing their jobs. They may also feel it is inappropriate and unprofessional. The second reason is personal. Many leaders don't consider themselves funny, don't understand the value of humor, and don't know how to incorporate fun into work.

The first reason is simply a misconception. Humor does not undermine work. To the contrary, it enhances an associate's ability to perform. Humor provides a physical and emotional release, a distraction from negative emotions, such as anger or stress, and it enables us to see challenges from a different perspective. Laughter is contagious: it elevates the mood of those around us and creates a positive social interaction. Whether one associate is having a bad day or a team of associates is facing a difficult situation at work, laughter will temporarily divert attention away from the problem. The diversion will likely improve their ability to cope with the challenge. According to Weinstein, the positive effects of fun can penetrate into the "heart and soul" of an organization:

> For too many companies, building a team means creating a high-powered, smoothly functioning organization that has plenty of muscle, but not much heart. It is the absence of the human side of business that depletes employee morale, and contributes to job dissatisfaction and burnout. By adding an element of fun and celebration to a team-building program, you can take an important step toward humanizing your workplace and creating a sense of heart and soul in your organization.[42]

Humor in the workplace involves some risk. By incorporating humor, you lighten the tone of the work environment. If this is taken too far, it can spin out of control and result in reduced focus and productivity.

Humor also has the risk of falling flat or being offensive. Humor in the workplace is not about practical jokes and should absolutely not involve off-color or politically incorrect statements or behavior. As described by Warren Shepell, an HR consultant, "Humor has nothing to do with taking your job lightly, joking about your company not being a good place to work or joking about its products and services... Humor that works in the workplace has to do with attitudes."[43]

Humor Displays Humility

Attitude is the key concept in the humor principle. Leading with humble humility demonstrates to your associates you truly love them and consider yourself one of them. On the other hand, leaders who exhibit hubris convey the notion that they consider themselves superiors and thus are not likely to win their associates' loyalty and trust. Leaders who take themselves too seriously will be viewed as stern and unsympathetic, and as a result, the associates will be unhappy and stressed. Show you care about their health and happiness by lightening up and easing their stress with humor. If you truly love your associates, leading with humility and humor is the only option. The impact humor and lightness has on the leaders themselves is equally important. Leaders need to release stress, or they will not be able to make rational decisions, be receptive to their associates, or achieve their goals. Your health and well-being are just as important as your associates' in your mutual efforts to succeed.

Humor in the workplace can be as simple as keeping a smile on your face or cheering up an employee with a kind act and supportive words. David Granirer, who provides seminars on laughter in the workplace, defines appropriate humor as "acts involving some sort of surprise and/or exaggeration that make people feel good. Certainly this can take some form of joke telling, but it can also take many others. Leaving a cookie on a coworker's desk, giving an unexpected compliment, and sending an encouraging e-mail are all acts that involve some form of surprise and leave people feeling good."[44]

The second, personal, reason for adding humor requires leaders to make a conscious effort to develop a culture of fun in the workplace. There are countless ways to lighten the mood or cause a laugh, and you don't have to be a funny person to incorporate this element into your leadership role. Don't try to be a comedian if it's not your style; furthermore, the humor should not cross the line of what is appropriate in a professional environment. Your office is not a comedy club. It is a place where your associates should feel that it is fun to work. In many respects, using humor is simply behaving in a way that is humane: be supportive, nurturing, and caring.

How to Incorporate Humor in the Workplace
There is no formula for incorporating humor into your business. You, your organization, and the individuals who work there are unique. Therefore, the first step is to make a personal assessment of your own humor quotient. Ask friends and family to give you an honest assessment of your "fun factor." How and when do you most readily exhibit your humor? Use their feedback to determine ways in which you will feel at ease expressing your sense of fun and lightheartedness. If you are truly "humor-impaired," seek a mentor to help uncover your sense of humor. Look for humor in everyday situations, as well as in reading material and interactions with others. Compile a humor library of jokes, quotes, cartoons, bumper stickers, articles, and stories that make you laugh. In moments of stress, take time to read one of the items again and share it with your staff. The result of your humor will not only be a pleasure for your associates, it will help you to release tension and maintain a positive attitude.

The next step is to assess your associates' personalities and the level of humor they currently display in the workplace. Consider what type of humor will be well-received within the organization. Wearing a clown nose to a staff meeting might not garner laughs; but breaking the ice by telling a joke on yourself could set the group at ease. Gentle, self-deprecating humor is a way to demonstrate to others you are human.

By showing you don't take yourself too seriously, others will feel more relaxed and comfortable expressing themselves in your presence.

Establishing your own precedent for humor is essential, as you must lead by example. You can't expect your associates to embrace humor if you don't exhibit that behavior yourself. The individual personalities of your associates will be affected by your attitude as a leader, and their attitudes are likely to mirror your own. A funny, quick-witted associate will eventually save the jokes for after hours if you frown or fail to laugh along with the others. A shy, quiet associate is likely to lighten up and become more spirited if you display a sense of humor and participate in the fun. Fun doesn't function if it is not shared. This means that your personal commitment to the benefits of humor, and your own pleasure in sharing it, must be genuine. If you connect with your associates on a human level (and love them), you will instinctively want to celebrate their successes, share kind words, and alleviate tension. You will enjoy your role as a leader, and it will be evident in your attitude. As a result, you will elicit great attitudes and loyalty from your associates. If you feel isolated and lonely at the top, then your abilities as a leader will be severely compromised. The fun factor is not just for your team's benefit; it is for yours as well.

The attitudes and environment in your organization cannot be changed in a day. It takes time and should be approached in increments. Consider your typical routine as well as your staff's. In what ways can you introduce a surprise to break up the routine and make it a more pleasant place to work for everyone involved? If you have a weekly staff meeting in the conference room, consider holding it in a variety of different places. Invite the staff to meet at a local restaurant; when the weather is nice, set up chairs or blankets and sit outside. You can bring bagels to a morning meeting, or choose a different associate each week to order in a surprise snack for the team. If the group has to work especially late one evening to meet a deadline, send them all home with gift certificates for pizza delivery as a way to show your appreciation. Demonstrating your appreciation can take many forms, and the more creative you are, the more fun it will be. At Playfair, Weinstein likes to express his thanks by having flowers delivered anonymously to an associate. The accompanying note tells the recipient he or she is appreciated and should pass the flowers on in a half hour to a coworker he or she appreciates in kind. Such gestures are not expensive or grandiose, but they promote positive feelings and attitudes.

Convincing the Boss About Humor's Benefits

Many leaders have superiors of their own, and those bosses may not readily embrace the concept of humor in the workplace. Your boss may be set in the belief that work is "serious" business that doesn't include laughter and fun. You don't want to lose your job, but you also don't want to fail your associates by ignoring humor as a key leadership principle for success. A good start would be to have an honest conversation with your supervisor and tell him or her you have been reading literature to help you improve as a leader. Explain that experts and case studies have convinced you that humor leads to greater productivity and job satisfaction. Give examples of the ways in which levity helps people to feel better and thus perform better. Your boss will also need time to adjust, but hopefully your example will also lead to a change in attitude at the top of the organization.

As you and your staff become more comfortable with humor, you should share the responsibility of bringing humor into the workplace. Appoint a humor ambassador or ask everyone to make suggestions of ways that fun and levity can be incorporated into the work. If you make having fun at work a priority, you will discover countless ways to act on it, as well as countless rewards for your efforts. Weinstein sums it up: "Laughter and play on the job are not an end in and of themselves. They are a doorway, and entrée into being more human with the people we work with… the only way to keep a sense of fun and play in your work life is to consciously choose to make it a priority."[45]

One of the greatest benefits of humor is that it promotes right-brain, creative thinking. Laughter puts us at ease and permits creativity to reign. In *A Whack on the Side of the Head*, author Roger van Oech writes: "If necessity is the mother of invention, play is the father. It's when you're not taking yourself seriously that your defenses are down, your mental locks are loosened, and there is little concern with the rules, or being wrong."[46] Success is driven by innovation; and the "crazy" notions that are ultimately proven to be brilliant ideas most often arise from creative rather than analytical thinking.

Brainstorming sessions will be more productive when humor is involved, as it breaks down the barriers of self-consciousness. If there is no "right" answer, every thought or contribution is valid and welcome. Some leaders use jokes or props to lighten the mood and promote laughter; others use games or gags. The methods by which you bring humor to the table are personal choices; the only requirement is to laugh together and enjoy the fun. Laughter creates an energy and camaraderie that bridges gaps. You and your associates will be more comfortable with each other, more receptive to each other's thoughts, and more willing to share your "crazy" ideas.

Promoting Creative Thinking

One strategy for prompting creative thinking is to play the "yes and ..." game. It starts with one person tossing out an idea that can be practical or zany, and each person in turn has to add to the idea by saying "yes and," then adding something to it. For example, a leader might gather his creative team together to discuss ways to increase public awareness of the company. The first idea might be "We should host an event"; the next person might say, "Yes and it should have a memorable theme"; the next might say, "Yes and there should be a contest," etc. By having only "yes" replies, there is no fear of being wrong; furthermore, the spirit and nature of the session are based on fun. Even if the ideas become impractical as the chain of "yeses" continues, there will likely be a few suggestions or kernels of creativity that may ultimately lead to an "aha."

For associates to be able to participate in this sort of freestyle thinking and sharing, they have to be open to humor. Everyone knows how to laugh, but there are some individuals who will find it challenging to lighten up and enjoy levity in the workplace. They may have the same fears that leaders have: that they won't be taken seriously or will appear unprofessional. It is the leader's responsibility to establish the humor precedent and help the associates to join in the fun. This is another aspect of associate development that is truly important for long-term success. Associates who can't learn to lighten up and maintain a healthy attitude will ultimately be those who turn over or burn out.

Is My Job Candidate Open to Humor?

In establishing a workplace that embraces humor, leaders also need to consider whether potential hires are a good fit in that environment. The tone of a job interview is typically serious, and candidates will most likely behave in a strictly professional manner. This presents a problem for leaders to gauge a candidate's humor quotient. To the extent that it is possible, try to put the candidate at ease and take note of whether the individual smiles often. If appropriate, tell a joke or humorous personal story and see if it elicits a laugh. When it is truly hard to assess whether a candidate can lighten up, address the issue openly. Explain that your team takes work seriously but laughter and fun are part of the culture. Ask the candidate if that is an environment in which he or she would be comfortable. Use the clues from body language, attitude, and dialogue to determine if an individual will mesh with your team and be able to participate in the fun.

When faced with difficult circumstances, your ability to use humor to diffuse stress and tension will actually help your associates to regain their focus and enthusiasm. We all try to organize our personal and professional lives so they run smoothly and don't negatively affect one another. Inevitably there will be times when family will take precedence and interfere with our plans at work. There are also times when work demands a personal plan to be sacrificed or put on hold. A loving boss recognizes that an associate's happiness and productivity involves more than what goes on at work. When a valued and reliable employee is simply having a bad day, respond in a way that is sensitive. Rather than a reprimand that will make the person feel worse, ease the tension through humor. Tell your associate to take a breather of some sort. If one associate is having a bad day, the negative attitude could affect other associates and lower their morale. It could also be evident to customers or clients. By helping the individual in distress, you also help the people who would be interacting with him or her.

Start with Your Comfort Zone

If you do not consider yourself funny or good at telling jokes, focus on your sense of humor and what makes you laugh. Start with your comfort zone, and then expand on it. Make it a personal challenge to seek out humor and come up with creative ways to share it with your associates. Remember, humor is not just "funny"; it includes unexpected gestures that are encouraging and kind. Following is a list of ways that you can begin to incorporate humor into your daily life and work:

- Set the example for your staff.
- Smile, laugh, be upbeat and friendly.
- Take every opportunity you can to find humor in the day-to-day events.
- Tell a joke on yourself.
- Find humor in travail; find humor in success.
- Break the ice with a funny anecdote.
- Hold brainstorming sessions in which funny, wacky, and crazy ideas are encouraged.
- Ask your associates for anonymous suggestions on ways to incorporate fun into their work, then select some and put them into practice.
- Designate a humor ambassador.
- Arrange an office contest for something silly such as the best self-portrait done with finger paint.
- Establish a casual attire day.
- Organize one fun outing each month.

- Create a welcoming ritual for new employees.
- Play "yes and ..." to promote creative ideas.
- Recognize when stress levels have reached a high and call a time-out.
- Take the staff to lunch.
- Order in a pizza.
- Send everyone outside for some fresh air.
- Hold staff meetings in a variety of locations.
- Break up the routine with a surprise.
- Take the staff to see a comedy film.
- Give each associate a joke-a-day calendar.
- Subscribe to an online humor newsletter.
- Humor involves elements of surprise, exaggeration, and fun. Think of ways to surprise your staff and encourage them to enjoy the moment.
- Seek out humor in your own life so that you feel comfortable when it's time to lighten up and elicit a laugh.
- Attend a comedy club show.
- Read the strange but true news at www.news.aol.com/strange.
- Play with kids as they are sure to make you laugh.
- Visit a toy store.
- Practice random acts of kindness.
- Have the staff spend a day doing charitable work because it promotes good feelings.
- Pay the toll for the car behind you and watch the driver's expressions of confusion and delight.
- Buy popcorn for the person in line next to you.
- Build a collection of funny cartoons, articles, bumper stickers, jokes, photos, and stories, and share it with others.
- Give a surprise gift of recognition that must be passed on.
- Send humorous cards to associates on special occasions.
- Celebrate the holidays with themed decorations and parties.
- Organize a staff retreat at an amusement park.

- Post a bulletin board with jokes, quotes, and cartoons.
- Create a humor zone at work and fill it with toys and games.
- Use silly props because they're so absurd they overcome our programming to behave like adults.
- Have a backup plan for jokes that fall flat, such as "the problem with that joke is that I outsourced the punch line to X" (X being the company's competitor).
- Take an improv class.
- The next time you laugh, make it so loud that everyone around you can hear it.

LINES YOU CAN LIFT

Self-deprecating for laughter...
"I'm such a poor speller the spell checker laughs at me."
"The ability to be cool under fire is a great skill. I wish I had it."
"As I once told (famous person), I can't stand name dropping."

When a joke bombs...
"Too bad, folks, that was the humor portion of the meeting."
"Some of these I just do for me. Bear with me."
(Look at notes) "It says here, 'Pause for laughter.'"[47]

It Helps to be Happy

Do you want to feel angry and stressed out, or do you want to feel positive and upbeat? The principle of humor should be an easy one to embrace, as we all want to be happy. Humor has a corollary effect on health, and the most significant factor that affects your ability to be a good leader is your physical and mental health. Your health impacts every aspect of your life, including your ability to enjoy your family, friends, hobbies, and activities outside of work. Humor is one of the most important areas in which you can truly nurture yourself.

Humor, as I am speaking of it, as it applies to leaders and to you as an individual, is not always about laughter or even "lightening up." An associate of mine recently took on a lot of personal commitments that limited the free time she previously had for her own activities during the evening. The problem, as she readily admits, is she is not a "morning person." Although she doesn't show up late, she is not one who would voluntarily suggest an early morning breakfast meeting. She prefers to have time before work to go through her morning routine without feeling rushed. Her routine includes reading the newspaper cover to cover, which is actually essential to her job and something she chooses to do before going to the office. She is also athletic and enjoys being physically active for the stress release as well as the health benefits.

When the demands on her time after work increased due to family obligations and her involvement with a local charity, she had no time left in the evening for exercise. The lack of exercise had a negative impact on her happiness. She felt stressed and disappointed in herself, as well as unhappy that she was missing out on something that gave her pleasure. A few months into her new, busier schedule, she realized she had to find a way to incorporate exercise back into her routine because it was an essential activity for her well-being. Now, her alarm rings an hour earlier, and she goes straight to the gym for a fifty-minute workout. Despite having to wake up so early, she says her attitude and outlook have improved tremendously because she starts the day by accomplishing something that makes her feel happy and good about herself. Furthermore, she says she is much more upbeat and relaxed at work when she has satisfied what is essential for her on a personal level.

The lesson in this story is that your ability to embrace humor and cope with stress can be improved if you make an honest assessment of your own personal needs and the things that make you happy. What are your hobbies? Do you enjoy playing sports, cooking, reading, watching movies, working for a charity, or simply spending time with friends and family? Whatever it is that makes you feel good and helps recharge your batteries should be given a priority in your daily routine. Sometimes circumstances change and there no longer seems to be a convenient time to fit those activities into the day. This is when you need to take a step back and reorganize your schedule. It is true that most people feel so many demands on their time that ultimately what they *want* to do is sacrificed for what they *must* do. In the long-term this is unhealthy, as it ignores the role that humor plays in our lives. If something that provides personal happiness and pleasure is made a priority, there is always a way to find time for it.

It is essential for you to identify a couple of personal priorities for yourself and then schedule them in your routine. When "self" priorities are set as appointments in your calendar, they are less likely to be ignored or delayed for when you "have time." You may need to adjust other activities in your schedule to accommodate your personal priorities, but in the long run, you will be a happier, healthier person who functions better at work as well as at home. The basis of humor is treating yourself as a human who requires understanding and nurturing.

Case Study—Barbara's Bad Day

Barbara works as a senior reporter for a local newspaper in a large city. The reporters and editors usually meet first thing in the morning to discuss the latest local developments, brainstorm on story ideas, and receive their daily reporting assignments. This morning the meeting was scheduled for earlier than usual. There was more to discuss due to an increase in the volume of news thanks to upcoming elections and a recent storm that had caused a lot of local damage. As a features writer for human interest stories, Barbara was responsible for interviewing some storm victims suffering from damage to their homes and power outages at their businesses.

When she was about to leave for work, her twelve-year-old son, David, announced he was sick and planning to stay home from school. She talked with him and realized he wasn't ill; he wanted to stay home in order to avoid a test in math class. After forty-five minutes of cajoling and threatening, she was able to drop David off and head to the office. Getting such a late start meant she was stuck in the worst of rush hour traffic, and she arrived at the newsroom well after the morning meeting had concluded. Barbara was a highly regarded reporter and conscientious employee, so it was upsetting for her to have personal issues affect her professional life. Furthermore, she knew she would have several new assignments for the day and would be under even more pressure to meet her deadlines.

She went directly to Jim, the managing editor, to apologize and find out what she had missed in the meeting. Jim was very understanding as he had worked with Barbara for several years and knew she would not be late without a legitimate reason. He reassured her he was sympathetic and had faced similar challenges with his own children. They discussed her assignments, and then Barbara went to her desk to begin making calls for interviews and checking facts for two of the stories that had been assigned to her. The newsroom was designed for the reporters, editors, and graphics team to openly interact, so Jim was able to see and hear what happened next.

Barbara began checking the facts an intern had researched for her story. There were several errors and inconsistencies. This meant she would have to spend even more time redoing the research herself. She called the intern over to her desk and reprimanded him in a way that was clearly humiliating to the young man. Ten minutes later, a woman she had planned to profile for a storm-related human interest piece called to say she didn't want the public attention and was backing out of the interview. Barbara was frantic, knowing she would have to start from scratch on both of these stories and therefore have to stay very late to finish her work. She thought of her son coming home from school to an empty house and started to feel as though she would break down in tears if her day continued like this. She simply couldn't handle the weight of her responsibilities and the pressure. Her head began to pound, and she couldn't even focus on what to do next.

From across the room, Jim observed Barbara deteriorate under the stress. He knew from experience that Barbara was strong and capable, but that she was human. He feared if her mood didn't improve she would continue lashing out at others just as she had done to the intern; however, *he was understaffed as it was and couldn't afford to send her home until she had completed the assigned stories.*

What can Jim do to diffuse the situation?

This is a perfect example of a time when humor and the human touch can be especially effective. Barbara was a valued and reliable employee who was simply having a bad day. Rather than reprimand her or make her feel worse about her predicament, Jim should ease her tension through humor. If he ignores the situation, he runs the risk she will lower others' morale by communicating poorly with them, the way she did with the intern. By helping Barbara, he also helps the people who interact with her. The best option is to help her lighten up and get over her bad mood.

Based on her late arrival, it is likely Barbara didn't have time for breakfast. Jim could go to a nearby deli and find something that would boost her energy as well as her spirits. Upon his return, the scenario might go something like this:

Jim goes to Barbara's desk and sets a lemon on it and says, "Barbara, this day has been a real lemon for you. I'm sorry it has been so rough, but you need to start over." With that, Jim pulls a lemonade out of a bag and sets that on her desk. Despite herself, Barbara starts to laugh, and it is such a welcome relief to break the tension. She realizes the world won't come to an end over one bad day. After sharing a laugh with her, Jim then hands over a bag with chips and a sandwich and kindly insists she take her lemonade and food to the lunch room and come back to her desk after she is nourished and ready to make a fresh start on the day.

Humor can take many forms, but the goal is to evoke pleasant feelings through unexpected or exaggerated acts of encouragement. A truly loving leader employs humor to lighten the mood and assist the associates in being healthy and productive.

CHAPTER NINE

INTEGRITY—Begin Every Action with a Commitment to Integrity

The rash of horrendous scandals that have plagued corporate America in recent times has put a spotlight on the integrity, and lack thereof, among today's business leadership. Seldom in the history of the twentieth and now in the early twenty-first century has there been a period of time in which corporate travesties of this nature have captured the attention of the American public. The result has been a huge loss of public confidence in corporate leadership. Leaders in corporate America are now ranked near the bottom on evaluations of trust and respect, even lower than politicians. This situation has created severe angst in corporate boardrooms and has incited a strong determination to regain the trust that American consumers once had.

Many in corporate America protest that the current public opinion resulted from just a handful of corporate leaders who made serious missteps and that the rest of the leadership community has been unfairly tainted by those mistakes. Indeed, only a small number of leaders have been accused, indicted, and convicted of corporate malfeasance; however, that does not disprove the view that the leadership of America's business community cannot be trusted.

A large segment of our society has concluded that the typical corporate leader follows the Gordon Gekko philosophy of "greed is good." The same people tend to believe the pursuit of financial reward drives corporate leaders to do whatever it takes for the corporate compensation system to work in their favor and that their (potentially) short tenure as CEO or senior executive will be richly rewarded for the substantial risk they take in assuming that perilous position. Far too many CEOs face the prospect of a one- or two-year tenure and consequently arrange or negotiate terms of compensation systems that are not affected by the quality of their performance.

Unfortunately for corporate America, the erosion of corporate integrity has created a burden for all leaders that will be difficult to carry in the coming years. Once the public's trust is lost, it is a huge challenge to regain it. Time may heal the wounds, but scars will remain. Trust and mutual respect are fundamental to all human relationships. Without trust, our relationships with customers, shareholders, associates, and vendors will be difficult to sustain. When there is a basic level of trust, the parties to a business relationship behave much differently than when that trust does not exist. Trust allows us to have enjoyable and efficient relationships as we pursue our organizational goals.

At the heart of trust is the commitment from every individual in an organization to behave in ways guided by a commitment to integrity. Our conduct must adhere at all times to the highest moral principles and professional standards. Truth, honesty, and fairness are not optional; they are mandatory. It may be challenging and occasionally unpleasant, but behaving with integrity is the only way to build trust and achieve success. Integrity and the trust it inspires provide great comfort to those who have business relationships with us. A breach of integrity forces our business partners to rely on testing and other controls that would be unnecessary if they had implicit trust in our behavior.

Leaders must build relationships founded on a commitment to integrity. Unfortunately, our society makes that commitment difficult. It appears, even to the casual observer, that standards of integrity in our society have changed dramatically over the years. Under the traditional rules of early America, integrity was a core value of the society. Those were the days when a handshake or verbal commitment would be honored. Some believe the secularization of our society has diminished the impact of the moral and ethical standards established by the commitment to a religious belief. The "absolute truth" standard seems to have given way to the more "nuanced" view that answers are not simply right or wrong, but rather much more "gray." The transparency of our society, with the media constantly watching and listening to every word, has caused politicians to avoid "telling it like it is" and opt instead to "spin the truth." Most of us are so accustomed to political spin we seldom expect the words we hear to be a fully accurate reflection of the truth. A true commitment to integrity would require that we never spin anything.

Some argue one breach of integrity by a leader can destroy any trust associates might have. Others argue it is our ongoing pattern of behavior that determines how we are perceived. There is no doubt some people find it difficult to accept any misjudgment they perceive to be a breach of integrity. In a discussion on leadership and integrity at the Wharton Business School, Kenneth I. Chenault, chairman and CEO of American Express, said, "If your people believe you have the right values, they will tolerate a few mistakes. In fact, they will stay with you. They want to see that you are decisive and compassionate, because they are asking people to take risks, to take chances. But don't confuse compassion with a reluctance to act decisively when necessary."[48]

Leaders must balance their commitment to integrity and their commitment to love. Often leaders tell substantially less than the "whole truth" so as to avoid jeopardizing the psychological well-being of one of their associates. In the guise of caring and sensitivity, leaders may mask the full, candid, and potentially hurtful truth when communicating with their associates. Such caring is not love, and it often stems from fear that the truth will have painful consequences. Love demands the truth, and leaders must exercise their commitment to integrity if they are to be effective in their application of love during virtually every interaction they have with their associates. A candid counseling session only has meaning when the "candor" is expressed with love. Candor without love can be brutal and hurtful.

Fear can influence a leader's willingness to be candid or direct with associates during discussions about their performance. Leaders may fear reprisal from their associates, or they may be concerned their associates have legitimate reasons to question, doubt, or even aggressively challenge the accuracy of the observations. How many times have you as a leader provided feedback to an individual and found the subsequent conversation more painful than it would have been had you remained silent? Leaders who have had this sort of experience may try to avoid such difficult conversations in the future. In so doing, they fail to effectively lead (and love) their associates and the organization. If an associate does not receive your honest feedback, whether positive or negative, the result is the associate is being led with anxiety rather than love. The loving thing to do is to provide feedback that helps your associates find ways to improve their performance or behaviors.

An entire organization suffers when leaders fail to have candid, direct, and meaningful conversations with their associates. Organizational performance reflects the sum total of individual performers in the organization. The leader is ultimately accountable for the quality of that performance. When a leader fails to provide meaningful feedback that is truly of the highest integrity, the organization is cheated of the potential for improved performance. Excellence cannot be achieved without the commitment to continually improving each individual's performance. It is the leader's responsibility to use every leadership tool available to maximize the performance against expectations set by the organization and its leaders. Leaders who have the highest standards of integrity understand this obligation to the organization and, irrespective of their contemplated fears, commit to taking high integrity actions.

What Is Integrity?

That old expression that says, "I may not be able to define it, but I know it when I see it" applies to integrity. There are probably as many definitions of integrity as there are speakers and writers on the subject. In Webster's dictionary, integrity is defined as:

1. firm adherence to a code of especially moral or artistic values: INCORRUPTIBILITY
2. an unimpaired condition: SOUNDNESS
3. the quality or state of being complete or undivided: COMPLETENESS

Maintaining a commitment to integrity in each and every one of our actions is a tough standard. I define integrity as doing the right thing, the honest thing, all the time and always for the right reasons. High integrity behavior is sometimes easy, but doing the right thing can be difficult when the cost of an action appears to be greater than the benefit of maintaining integrity. It is easy to tell the truth when the truth is already known by the questioner. It is much more difficult to answer a question truthfully when doing so has an obvious downside. If I tell my boss I slept in, rather than create a story about horrible traffic in the wake of a car accident, that truth could damage my career. My boss may think I have no discipline and cannot wake up in time to get to work. The truth may set you free, but in this case that freedom could be job loss.

Integrity means we should always tell the truth, and not just when it feels good or is easy. We also need to do it for the right reasons. Telling the truth, or what is perceived to be the truth, is important, but the motivation should not be self-serving. As an example, if it is true that a rival for your next promotion is a liar, to say so because you want to destroy his or her career is not an action based in integrity. The right reason matters.

We also need to be able to learn how to tell the truth. A commitment to integrity in the first instance might be to tell the truth in a way that also explains the other mitigating circumstances that caused you to oversleep. In the second example, we might be obligated to tell the truth in a way that does not destroy the person, even if that means providing a reasonable rationale as to why the individual has never before exhibited this flaw; it might be a simple mistake.

During his discussion at Wharton, Chenault described integrity as the single most important attribute and principle of leadership. He defines integrity as being honest, as well as being consistent in words and actions. Without strong values and actions that are consistent with those values, a leader will ultimately not succeed. He also addressed the scandals that have recently plagued corporate America and how these incidents highlighted the need for leaders to behave according to the highest moral and ethical standards. "Today, the stakes are incredibly high," Chenault said. "The need for leaders to stand for something and act from principle is more important than ever. Things that were acceptable five or 10 years ago will today cost you your career… if you are not clear on who you are, on what you stand for, and if you don't have strong values, you are going to run your career off a cliff."[49]

A Culture of Integrity?

Have you ever worked for an organization whose values you thought were flawed? What did you do? Did you stay and just ignore the circumstances? Did you quit? This is a tough issue, and there are no easy answers.

The dilemma we frequently face in the arena of ideas is there are many views, philosophic or simply opinion, that differ. If I am a current-day political conservative, I probably believe in the primacy of the individual and individual initiative. On the other hand, if I am a political liberal, I value the use of society to support the weak individuals collectively. These two positions establish likely behaviors and set up potential conflict for any individual who might have a view of society that differs from the one currently dominant in the political party in power. This difference in views has much to do with the political arguments we hear in a variety of public media. Which side is correct? On a more abstract level, this question cannot be answered. If I believe in the position of the conservative, then I am convinced I am right and that the society should follow the path that flows from my conviction. The other side of the argument is wrong, in the conservative opinion, and vice versa.

The core lesson here is you do not need to have an untruth to create an integrity problem. A simple disconnect between the values of an organization and those of the individual could result in an integrity violation. Consider an organization with extensive behaviors that prove to you it does not honor its customers. You come to that conclusion because you see the organization always charges the highest price the market will bear. You, on the other hand, have a deep sense that all organizations must be committed to offering customers the very best service at the very best price. How do you reconcile the organization's behavior with your own value?

In this case, a classical economist could easily conclude that the organization has a core value of profit maximization and it actually has an obligation to its shareholders to charge the highest price the market will bear. Hence, the behavior of charging the highest price would be consistent with a core value of the enterprise, and yet violate your sense of values.

According to your value of fairness, the corporation should charge a lower price and certainly not always all the market can bear. If you believe strongly in this value, you could potentially find yourself troubled by the organization's decision making and might even view it as evidence the organization has low integrity. Ironically, an organization with this profit maximization goal would probably believe anybody not working toward maximizing shareholder profit would be committing a breach of integrity.

Our philosophy on values and the core concepts of right and wrong may differ, but each of us in the workplace will eventually be faced with situations that require value-based decisions. There will be times when our personal values appear to conflict with the organization's values. When they do, we will inevitably be faced with the need to reconcile that conflict, resolve it, ignore it, or walk away from it. The irony is many organizations do not have a clear expression of their values, and consequently, their employees or prospective employees have no way of knowing if the corporation's values conflict with their own personal values.

As an individual with a set of values, it is imperative you understand as much as possible about the organization's values before you join it, because if there is a wide disparity, it will cause you great conflict and pain.

A conflict of values is difficult to resolve. If you have a strong commitment to a value that is inconsistent with an organization's values, it may actually be a personal violation of integrity for you to remain in the organization. The organization also would probably be better off if all those who did not subscribe to its values were to leave. Indeed, any employee who did not behave consistently within the value structure probably would be viewed as creating an integrity breach.

Can a Leader Behave with a Commitment to Integrity Despite a Lack of Organizational Integrity?

The simple answer to this question is "yes!" My behavior does not need to be controlled by anybody else but me. I am responsible for my level of commitment to integrity, so if I believe in a set of values, then I can and should do what I believe to be right, irrespective of the organization's views. If I truly believe, then I will not be distracted from my path.

In theory, our individual beliefs should dictate our behavior; however, we are undeniably influenced by the "tone at the top." It is clear that what an organization's top leadership establishes as the norm of behavior will eventually become the norm within the organization. If the culture at the top of Enron was one that said, "Do the deal, no matter what the cost," then every person in the organization would have been influenced by that culture. The senior leaders of an organization may not fully realize it, but their impact on others is enormously powerful.

So, what can I do as a leader if I do not believe in the "kill for the deal" culture? Can there be a "sub-culture" that says, "Not all deals are worth doing if they harm others"? One could argue that, if I believe in my principles, I will prevail. But the corrosive nature of the described culture would make it virtually impossible to survive in that type of organization without acquiescence to the organization's values. Eventually, the contradicting value will be expunged by the leadership behavior and, in particular, the reward system. If the leaders value "cutthroat competition," then that is the behavior they will reward, and eventually that is the behavior they will get. Any "rogue" ideas by members of the organization will be driven out.

Let's go back to the question "Can a leader value integrity in an organization that does not?" The answer is "yes, but not for long." If an individual leader behaves in a way that is inconsistent with the acceptable behavior, eventually that leader will change behavior and become "one of them." Or the individual will fail by the organization's standards and will leave or be fired. Ultimately, the realistic and highly pessimistic answer to the question is "no!" Call it the "Law of Bad Leadership": bad leaders at the top will drive out good leaders at the bottom. Eventually, the organization will end up with only those who sell out to a lack of integrity or those who never had any in the first place.

Is There Hope for High Integrity Leaders?

The negative conclusion of the previous section should not be where we leave the discussion of integrity. There is little doubt high integrity leaders should have a strong commitment to integrity, and therefore, we cannot assume they will be unable to change an organization from within. The previous section sounds like a particularly pessimistic view of changing an organization with rotten values. The good news is organizations can change, and recent studies reflect that American corporations are increasing efforts to improve their cultures. According to the 2005 *National Business Ethics Survey*, which surveyed more than 3,000 American workers, 69 percent of employees said their companies implement ethics training, which is a 14 percentage point increase from 2003.[50]

Tragically, much of the change that occurs in organizations, as in the world of politics, results from a crisis. Often the behavior predicated on the lack of integrity encourages or precipitates a crisis. Many organizations have found a way out of a crisis because leaders, either from within or from without, have committed to change. If the crisis is severe enough, the entire culture can be shocked into a dramatic shift. It is important the cancer of lost integrity is not so pervasive that the organization is populated by only the weak or the flawed. One example of an organization that lost its way at the top is Hewlett-Packard (HP). This organization has very high standards and a rich culture of commitment to a value system known as the "HP Way." It appears much of the culture remained intact, but not at the top.

The tragic story of HP's apparent illegal practice called "pre-texting" demonstrates that even an organization known for its virtuous business ethics can be polluted by a breach at the top. The scandal that ensued caused many to leave the board and the organization, and several individuals, including the former chair of the board of directors, were indicted in California. Those individuals appeared to have strayed from the company's tradition of sound values and integrity. However, the strong culture that exists deep into the organization has reportedly survived and seems to be working with the new leadership to save the company from demise.

The HP story suggests that an ethical culture at the bottom of an organization can eventually prevail. If integrity is a value that has positive influence on the organization, then hopefully, the lack of an integrity culture at the top will eventually lead to an organization's failure. If that is true, then the good leaders at the bottom can overcome the "bad leader" at the top, hence invalidating the Law of Bad Leadership. The mission of restoring integrity within an organization may be influenced by its size, complexity, and geographic dispersion, but it can be accomplished more easily when the top fails than when the entire organization fails.

Some organizations manage to mask their lack of integrity for a surprisingly long time. The Enron story is once again a perfect example. Enron had been the darling of the investment community for decades, and it took a financial crisis to bring the house of cards down. In the case of WorldCom, it took the courage of an internal auditor to speak up and tell the Board Audit Committee she thought there was "something wrong" with the accounting. In the final analysis, neither Enron nor WorldCom survived as stand-alone entities. The message is clear: eventually the "bad guys" get caught, but it is difficult for outsiders to see that a corporate culture lacks integrity. The good leaders from within must be the organization's salvation and cause others to commit to the value of integrity.

There Are Good Leaders, and There Is Hope

A leader who exemplifies high integrity is Jon M. Huntsman. He started as an entrepreneur in 1970. By 2000 he had grown his company, Huntsman Corp., to the largest privately held petrochemical and plastics business in the world. He is widely recognized for his excellence in leadership as well as his philanthropy, and has been honored with numerous awards, including the 2001 Entrepreneur of the Year Award. When his company went public in 2005, it had annual revenues in excess of $12 billion and operations in forty-four countries. That same year, Huntsman wrote the book *Winners Never Cheat: Everyday Values We Learned as Children (But May Have Forgotten)*.

Huntsman's story demonstrates that success and integrity go hand-in-hand. The book is based on his personal business experiences, which serve as a moral compass for other leaders. His principles include "competing fiercely and fairly, but no cutting in line" as well as "the importance of surrounding oneself with associates who listen to their conscience and act accordingly; and of treating customers, colleagues, employees and competitors with respect."[51] Following is an excerpt from the third chapter, "Play by the Rules."

> Which rules we honor and which we ignore determine personal character, and it is character that determines how closely we will allow our value system to affect our lives... Character is most defined by integrity and courage. Your reputation is how others perceive you. Character is how you act when no

one is watching. These traits, or lack thereof, are the foundation for life's moral decisions. Once dishonesty is introduced, distrust becomes the hallmark of future dealings or associations… Businessmen and women do not place their integrity in jeopardy by driving hard bargains, negotiating intensely, or fiercely seeking every legitimate advantage. Tough negotiations, however, must be fair and honest. That way, you never have to remember what you said the previous day… Once you compromise your values by agreeing to bribes or payoffs, it is difficult ever to reestablish your reputation or credibility. Therefore, carefully choose your partners, be they individuals, companies or nations.[52]

The advice to choose carefully is particularly relevant when evaluating the integrity of a potential employee or employer. It is not an easy task, as uncovering an individual's or organization's true character generally takes time. How can a leader who spends only a couple hours in interviews with a potential associate determine if that individual has high standards of integrity? There are several steps an employer can take to ensure that it attracts and hires people committed to integrity. As often repeated in this chapter, it begins with your own behavior. Act with integrity in all of your leadership and business activities, and you will gain a reputation as one who has excellent moral and ethical character. This reputation will attract others who share your high standards. If your organization does not already have a statement of values and ethics, suggest that one be created. This statement should define the behavior and ethics critical to the organization's culture of integrity. Each member of the organization should have a printed copy of the statement, and it should be posted on the company's Web site to demonstrate to potential customers and employees that the company is committed to integrity.

In the interview process, the statement of values and ethics can be handed to candidates as a way to initiate a discussion of how important integrity is in your organization. Candidates who do not share that belief are likely to be uncomfortable and may realize the job is not the right fit. Another tactic for assessing character is to ask behavior-related questions such as how they have handled difficult problems or customers. You could also ask the candidates to give examples of goals they set and how they went about accomplishing them.

When you are ready to make a job offer, take the time to verify the accuracy of a résumé and check references. Ask previous employers about the person's responsibilities, contributions, attitude, and interaction with others. Some references will be more forthcoming than others, but hopefully you will learn enough to support or disprove your sense that the candidate has high ethical standards and will fit in your organization's culture.

For those who are seeking a new job, it is equally important and challenging to determine if your potential employers are truly committed to integrity. Start by researching the company. Read the organization's Web site thoroughly and check for a position statement. Do an online search and look for news items and press releases that shed light on the organization's social responsibility, financial practices, and internal culture. Gauge the organization's reputation by talking to others who work in the same industry or have been clients or customers. During an interview, ask questions that illuminate aspects of integrity, such as whether there is a code of ethics and what the organization's priorities are. If you receive a job offer, it is also fair for you to request references so you can speak with others who will hopefully confirm your belief that this is an organization with high standards of integrity. Your goal is to join an organization in which every individual believes in the value of integrity and behaves accordingly.

The responsibility of a leader to act as a coach and mentor was discussed in the chapter on associate development. In regards to the subject of this chapter, it is important for leaders to find their own "integrity" mentors. Those mentors can be at the senior level as well as at a relatively low level in the organization's structure. The goal is to form relationships with individuals whom you admire for their ethical and moral behavior. When faced with a difficult situation that requires you to make a value-based decision, you will not have to depend solely on your own ethics and morals. The advice of your mentors will support or challenge your sense of the right thing to do. By sharing the burden of ensuring integrity, you are also strengthening the culture of commitment to integrity. To succeed as a leader, always remember that success and integrity go hand-in-hand.

Everybody who strives to be a responsible and honorable corporate citizen wants to know what it means to behave with a "commitment to integrity." As you might suspect, that is both a simple question to answer and, at times, can seem an impossible challenge to live up to. The simple answer is to always do the right thing, no matter how tempting it is to compromise your values of right and wrong. But such a simplistic rule is nearly meaningless when we are faced with "real world" challenges.

VALUES THREATS

Here are some "real world" tips on how to decide what to do in a situation that challenges your values:

- It may seem obvious, but when faced with a question of fact, always tell the truth. That means, if somebody asks you to outright lie, do not, no matter what the rationale.

- When faced with a question about a colleague at work, avoid value judgments about his or her behavior or personality. The best way to avoid a dishonest or a "short on integrity answer" about your associates is to simply say, "I do not gossip or talk about people." It does not mean you should not have an opinion; it does mean you should keep those kinds of opinions to yourself. The benefit: you do not hurt somebody, and you are not forced to say nice things that you don't honestly believe.

Values Threats (con't)

- Be candid, not cruel. It is possible to be critical without hurting a person or an organization. When giving leadership feedback, think how you would react to the same feedback.
- Never knowingly go to work for an organization that has low standards of integrity or ethics. If you discover that weakness, get a new job. Cultures with low standards of integrity and ethics always become hostile to those who choose to live by a higher standard.
- Never tolerate a breach of integrity in your own behavior. It is imperative to set the standard for your staff. The concept of "tone at the top" has no tolerance for the old saw "Do as I say, not as I do." As Huntsman writes, "Children observe their elders so they know how to act. Employees watch supervisors. Citizens eye civic and political leaders. If these leaders and role models set bad examples, those following frequently follow suit. It's that simple."[53]
- Never tolerate breaches of integrity in your organization. Set a high standard of expectations, and hold those who fail fully accountable. You may choose to forgive, but you should never ignore misdeeds. Your staff needs to know you will not tolerate a failure to behave ethically. Punishment may not be appropriate, but clear and unambiguous "corrective action" must be taken.
- Avoid the temptation to compromise on core values, just because it is convenient.

Case Study—Martha Forgets Integrity; Be Honest with Yourself

Integrity has been called the "single most important attribute" of leaders. A combination of many attributes can be identified as those great leaders possess, just as many attributes combined can make someone a great friend, spouse, business partner, or associate. The one common factor in each of those combinations is integrity. If an individual lacks integrity, he or she cannot be trusted, admired, relied upon, or respected. He or she simply cannot be "great" in the minds of those who have sound moral and ethical values.

If your personal adherence to integrity is sound, you probably act instinctively at work and don't have to give much thought to making "right" decisions that are honest, fair, and ethical. It is likely your moral compass guides you and doesn't require serious attention except in times when you are faced with an ethical crisis that might have been brought on by the behavior or decisions of others. Because our personal integrity is taught and ingrained in most of us very early in our lives, it is something we don't have to work on or improve each day, and thus we generally take it for granted. When challenged by others or put into situations that require us to make an integrity-based decision, we have to take the time to consider what adheres to our own values. Rarely are we required to think about and apply integrity to our "selves." As a result, we may neglect to be fair, honest, and loyal to ourselves.

Personal integrity includes not just how we interact with others but also how we interact with ourselves. It is easy to accept the responsibilities and activities that occupy our days without periodically stepping back and making an honest assessment about whether they are in harmony with who we are as individuals. When did you last seriously think about whether you are personally fulfilled and what you can do to help yourself reach or maintain that feeling? Are you setting personal goals, and are you achieving them? What matters most to you in life, and are you nurturing it? Maintaining personal integrity requires a conscious inner dialogue that will keep us loyal to our own values. Only when we are honest and loyal to ourselves will we be able to fulfill our greatness as individuals of every nature.

ARE YOU HONEST WITH YOURSELF?

Answer these questions *honestly*. Do you …

* truly love your job?
* feel personally fulfilled?
* feel proud of yourself and your achievements?
* consider yourself successful in the ways that matter most to you?
* meet your own expectations? exceed them?
* meet your boss's expectations? exceed them?
* nurture your personal needs and pursue your passions?

Martha is the vice president of operations at a start-up technology company headquartered in Silicon Valley. She has had several jobs in the software industry and has actually held similar positions in two other start-ups. One turned out to be a true success; the other was a complete bust. Much of the latter experience was very unpleasant, and she knows it left scars which have yet to fully heal. She invested a good deal of money into the second company, and within eighteen months, the company closed its doors. Adding insult to injury, she discovered the company's CEO had lied to virtually every investor about the state of the company and was essentially a fraud who squandered most of the cash invested by the venture capital firms.

Martha was devastated by the experience and swore she would never again make that type of mistake. She committed to researching the principles in her next firm and did just that before accepting her current position. She spent a good deal of time talking to people who had worked with, and for, the current CEO, and she was convinced he was of the highest integrity.

Martha signed on about ten months ago, and she put her full energy into the job. She hired many of the same people who had worked for her at the previous "failed firm" and felt she had assembled a great team. The company had a vision similar to her last company's, so it was easy for her to be excited and to recruit those who had been great employees at the previous company.

Over the last three months, Martha developed serious reservations about her current CEO. There were subtle (but to her mind, clear) signs he was making expenditures on wasteful and self-serving trips, equipment, and even what she saw as personal "lifestyle perks." She was not in a position to be monitoring expense patterns, but she was convinced money was misused in a way that reminded her of what she had seen in the last company.

Martha knew the CFO of her company pretty well and about a month ago decided to mention her concerns to him. After her conversation (which she pleaded he keep confidential), she had an uneasy feeling the CFO was not very receptive to her anxiety. Her fears were then quickly confirmed when she was called into the office of the CEO and confronted with her "allegations." The meeting was pretty heated, and by the time it was over, she found herself "repenting" and apologizing to the CEO for even the hint of distrust.

Since that meeting, her relationship with the CEO had clearly changed, and Martha found herself distanced from much of the core decision making. She also had several more experiences that reinforced her concerns the CEO was not being an effective steward of the investors' money. She has now concluded that the situation will damage the company, but she feels terribly uncertain and conflicted as to what her next step should be.

Martha is at a crossroads; what should she do?

Martha has every reason to feel conflicted. From what we know, there is an overwhelmingly strong case for her to be certain there are spending improprieties. One the other hand, her previous experience has made her understandably "gun shy" about the warning signs she sees. It is not clear that she has enough evidence to go forward with an allegation of impropriety or fraud. It is clear that she has very few options: 1) do nothing, meaning stay and ignore the problem; 2) find another job and resign; 3) stay and continue to monitor the behavior of the CEO, even conduct her own "investigation"; 4) report her findings to one or more members of the board of directors and/or investors.

The first option is unfortunately the one many people take. This is tragic because it means the individual has essentially "condoned" the behavior, as well as sacrificed his or her individual sense of integrity. I do not support that action because it is one of the reasons why so many of corporate America's scandals went unstopped. Too many times, the employees knew something was wrong, yet they did nothing about it.

The second option is clearly a possibility. If the environment at the company makes the employee uncomfortable, then an action to eliminate that discomfort is reasonable. In this case, Martha tried to alert the financial control point, and that failed to produce a reasonable result. It would be easy to understand if Martha decided the best course of action for her would be to move on before the company "blows up."

The third action, or some version of it, is probably the one that most people would opt for in the short-term. Assessing whether there is "evidence" of malfeasance is a reasonable course. The challenge for Martha will be that the work climate is already tense, so she may find it difficult to obtain documented "facts" that could be used to report the improprieties. It is also a challenge to determine where she should report the facts, in the event that she actually uncovers evidence.

The last action is theoretically the correct action, but it is fraught with risk. If Martha turns to any of the directors and investors, and they in turn break her confidence as the CFO did, then there is little hope for her to have a career in the organization. On the other hand, if she does report it, and they honor the request, then the truth might be determined by independent actions of the board and/or investors.

All of that said, what would I advise Martha to do? I recommend she do several things in sequence. She should stay and continue to monitor, because what she has reported thus far is mostly anecdotal and conjecture. It is advisable for her to try to find clear evidence, one way or the other. She should also begin to evaluate alternative job opportunities. If my relationship with the CEO had become noticeably strained, I would want to move on, as it may not be possible to get past what he views as a breach of trust.

Remember, if Martha is wrong about her fears, then she has "wrongfully accused" her boss. It is hard to get over that.

Finally, I would hold open the option of going to the board/investor group. Should she find concrete evidence, or find another job, she should probably attempt to alert those people quickly. My sense of integrity would not allow me to just quit and walk away. I would feel an obligation to alert somebody there might be a problem. If this were a public company, the securities regulations require there be a "hotline" to which potential "whistle blowers" can provide their thoughts. I am the chairman of the Audit Committee of several companies, and in each instance, we have a system to allow people to come forward with these kinds of suspicions.

CHAPTER TEN

PASSION—Drives Purpose and Performance

Passion is a driving force in the human spirit, and when passion is present, success is attainable. Where passion is lacking, success will be lacking as well. If leaders don't deeply believe in all aspects of their work and don't feel passionately about their business, they will lack commitment and creativity. Passion stimulates energy, desire, confidence, and faith in the ability to achieve extraordinary results. It also fuels the determination to overcome obstacles and cements the conviction that it can be done. Many of the leadership principles involve actions you must take; passion is a force that must be felt for you to be a successful leader.

To understand how passion affects our behavior, consider reading a book you love versus one you don't. Some books you will pick up and not be able to set down until you finish; others will take weeks and you may never get to the end. The difference is the emotional commitment you feel to the books you love. The same is true for an assignment at work. If you love doing it, you will finish it quickly and do a better job at it than if it is an assignment you dislike or merely tolerate. Passion is what makes us unfailingly committed to getting the results we want, whether it's making a personal relationship last, winning a competition, or achieving greatness on the job. Passion creates purpose, and if you are filled with passion and purpose, you will overcome every challenge in your path to success.

An extraordinary performance almost always requires an extra expenditure or energy. To excel on the job, it may require studying, putting in longer hours, learning something new (possibly something you don't find interesting), traveling, or sacrificing personal time for work. If you believe in the big picture and have passion for what you are doing, then you will be able to get through the less enjoyable parts with considerably less pain. If you don't have passion for your job, it will be extremely painful, and ultimately, you won't succeed. Leaders who just "get by" or survive will not live up to their own potential, and they will not inspire their associates to live up to their potential either. Employees inevitably reflect the attitudes of their employers, so your passion or lack of it has an enormous impact on your staff.

If you have ever been a sports fan, you know about the power of passion. In sports, it is typically called emotion. You can see how emotion (passion) impacts the outcome of sports almost every time you participate in or observe the flow of a game. The success or failure of most teams is also impacted by the natural capabilities, knowledge, and skills of the players, but the end result of competition is driven much more by emotion. Most of the teams in the National Football League (NFL) or the National Basketball Association (NBA) are well-balanced with players of comparable skills. There are a few exceptions such as the phenomenal quarterbacks Brett Favre and Peyton Manning, basketball giant Shaquille O'Neal and superstar Michael Jordan, but by and large, on any given day any team could win.

The obvious differentiator is the role of emotion, and in sports, that emotion usually increases the amount of adrenaline flowing. Coaches encourage this by "pumping up" their teams with emotional speeches. The players then sustain that emotion with screams and enthusiastic celebrations at every success. Their emotions may stem from anger at the foe, anger at the prospect of losing, fear of the coach's anger, or even excitement at the prospect of winning. Whatever the emotion, when the team is "pumped up," they often win, regardless of their skill level. It is not always the better team that wins, but rather the team that has the highest emotional investment.

In the world of work, emotion does not play precisely the same type of role, but it plays a role nonetheless. It is seldom the reality that the work team is infused with huge amounts of emotion-induced adrenaline, but emotion does generate a new kind of reaction. The difference is in the world of work, we are not limited to sixty minutes of playing time. Instead, we are expected to sustain our passion over an extended period of time. Raw emotion, which generates the adrenaline rush, cannot be sustained, so in the workplace we must have a substantially different mechanism to drive performance that exceeds the norm and expected level of success. In this case, the better term to define emotional impact is *passion*. Passion plays the same type of role in the world of work that adrenaline plays in sports. In order to achieve sustained winning performance, we must have the passion to achieve outstanding performance.

So what is passion? The dictionary offers a variety of definitions:

1. Any powerful or compelling emotion or feeling, as love or hate.
2. Strong amorous feeling or desire; love; ardor.
3. Strong sexual desire; lust.
4. A person toward whom one feels strong love or sexual desire.
5. A strong or extravagant fondness, enthusiasm, or desire for anything: a passion for music.
6. The object of such a fondness or desire: Accuracy became a passion with him.
7. An outburst of strong emotion or feeling: He suddenly broke into a passion of bitter words.
8. Violent anger.

Obviously, the definitions focused on sexual desire are not relevant. But further down the list we have the key to understanding the type of passion we need in the world of work … "a strong or extravagant fondness, enthusiasm, or desire for anything: a passion for music." In the case of an employee, it is a passion to live by the organization's values and to achieve the organization's goals.

That does not tell the whole story. Passion is something we feel in our psyches, or in our souls. It is an emotion deep inside us that says, "I believe so much in the core values and goals that I will not let anything stop me from pursuing and achieving those goals." It is an emotion driven from belief, not a belief driven from emotion or from adrenaline. This type of motivation to achieve is uniquely human and reflects the best in us as members of our species.

Our passion to win is not enough; we must have the passion to achieve the organization's goals. Achieving a winning record as a leader requires a passion that drives us to perform exceptionally and to exceed goals. Passion is the work life equivalent of adrenaline in sports. There is no doubt a belief in an organization's core values can energize us to further those beliefs, but only a passion to achieve organizational goals can drive us to achieve what to some will seem like the impossible.

Passion Is Power

Passion is genuine and cannot be "faked" for an extended period of time. Either you are fired up and enthusiastic about something or you are not. If you are truly passionate about your work, it is an incredibly powerful tool for success. The beauty of passion is that everyone can have it. You don't have to learn passion, or earn a degree in it; it comes naturally when your personal talents, interests, and motivational triggers coincide. As a leader, you need to hire people with the appropriate skills to fulfill the work, but it is also important to assess whether their interests and talents intersect with the organization's core mission, vision, and goals. When your associates have passion for their work, their motivation will come from within and they will require less supervision and perform better than those lacking passion. Furthermore, the associates with passion are those who can be groomed to become leaders themselves.

While there is no formula for identifying whether potential employees' passion coincides with the job, there are clues. Have they identified what their individual talents are? Do they understand what they really *want* to do as opposed to simply naming what they have done in previous jobs? Have they sought out work in a field or position that matches their personal interests? If individuals lack the drive or initiative to seek out employment that ensures their own happiness on the job, they are not likely to have the drive to help an organization succeed in its mission.

When it comes to hiring individuals to serve as leaders—not just subordinates—there are a number of factors to consider. Passion is undeniably one of the prerequisites. Jonathan Byrnes, a senior lecturer at Massachusetts Institute of Technology, attended a meeting with a top admissions officer for a leading graduate school of business. The admissions officer he spoke with, as he related in an article he later penned, was reviewing the profiles of students who had been accepted for the upcoming semester. One student's definition of leadership said: "Leaders are people who leave their footprints in their areas of passion."[54] Not only is this an incredibly poetic way to describe leadership, it also captures the essence of how important this role is and how monumentally influential a leader can be.

In the sports analogy, passion is equated with adrenaline. Passion in any aspect of our lives creates a "high" that is exciting and makes us feel enthusiastic, energetic, and upbeat. When passion is missing, there is a corollary "low" that may manifest itself as lethargy or apathy. Consciously or unconsciously, we crave the positive feelings passion brings with it. Therefore, if you or your associates are not passionate about your work, it is likely you will look for a different job to satisfy your craving. If you are not looking, you should be. According to leadership guru Stephen Covey, far too many people are not thriving at work and suffer from a lack of passion. He compares passion to finding your voice by tapping into your individual spirit, hope, and intelligence: "When you engage in work that taps your talent and fuels your passion—that rises out of a great need in the world that you feel drawn by conscience to meet— therein lies your voice, your calling, your soul's code."[55]

To be an effective leader, you must be passionate about your organization's mission, as well as your leadership role and responsibilities. You will not be able to influence or inspire your associates without a personal conviction in what you are trying to achieve. If you view leadership as an assignment imposed on you by the parameters of your job, as opposed to a calling to enable others to achieve greatness, you are in the wrong job. Leadership is about helping others to realize their extraordinary potential. The best leaders are not always the ones who can give the best speech or receive the most recognition from their superiors. The best leaders are the ones who can unite their team in a passionate commitment to achieve superior results for themselves as individuals and the organization as a whole.

The renowned leadership guru Warren Bennis describes good leaders as those who make everyone feel his or her contribution makes a difference in the organization, thus giving meaning to his or her work. Michele Payn-Knoper, a motivational leadership consultant and author, takes this notion and applies it to the passion principle:

> The "meaning" is essential to the happiness of an individual, whether they are working for a large corporation, volunteering for a non-profit, or developing their own business. After all, humans naturally desire to make a positive contribution to society; a lasting impact on both the present and future. I believe great leaders recognize that need, draw upon it, and use it to engage individuals in their cause. Essentially, they draw others to the flame of their passion.[56]

Leaders are the torch-bearers for passion, and the brighter the flames, the more likely their associates will be drawn to it and follow it. Influencing and leading your associates through passion is powerful. Unfortunately, the passion that drives strong leadership can be abused. A look back in history at the world's most memorable leaders demonstrates the incredible good as well as the horrific evil that their passions have inspired. For a modern-day example of that evil, we only need to think back to September 11, 2001. Be certain your passion and resultant power are channeled toward worthy goals. Wielding this power simply to satisfy your ego or achieve self-serving goals is wrong and defies everything that was discussed in the previous chapter about integrity.

Passion, like integrity, needs to be present from the top to the bottom of an organization. You should not expect your associates to feel passionately about the organization's mission and success if they do not see that passion in their leader. A positive spirit and attitude at the top will infuse the organization with energy and enthusiasm. It also inspires loyalty and confidence. If you can connect with the passion in your associates' souls, they will work to exceed your expectations even in the most challenging times.

Using Passion to Inspire

Using passion to inspire and influence your associates is different than using it to control them. The hope is that your passion will ignite their own passion so they feel motivated from within themselves and love their work as much as you do. The CEO of one of the largest HVAC distributors in the country, L.B. "Bud" Mingledorff, was interviewed about vision and passion in leadership. He said passion is actually a way to liberate workers in respect to how they view their jobs.

"Passion relates to energy and energy relates to really being able to get control of your life. When people think that someone else is in control of them then they don't have much passion. You have to teach people that their jobs are how they perceive it. They teach you in kung fu that competition is within you. What you're doing is you're competing with your inner self to become your very best. And if you can become passionate about that then how can you not be passionate about your job because it is you."[57]

Passion for work can take a variety of forms and means different things to different people. Some people are passionate about the work itself and the challenge to perform their best, while others are passionate about the organization's mission and the outcome or message that results from the work. One of my colleagues learned this lesson early in her career. After working for a boutique public relations firm that represented only a handful of clients in the film industry, she made a step "up" and was hired as an account manager for a large, full-service PR firm. The firm's clients included a wide variety of businesses and individuals seeking to promote themselves through positive publicity and recognition in the media. My colleague learned that working for so many diverse clients didn't appeal to her because she didn't believe in some of the clients' messages or value to the public. The lack of a passionate belief in these clients made the work unpleasant, and she struggled to perform her best on their behalf.

She eventually left to head the in-house PR department for a company whose mission she appreciated. As a result, she truly enjoyed her work and felt personally invested in the organization's success. My colleague learned an important lesson about herself and the way in which passion plays a role in her personality and her desire to perform. Finding a job with a company she believed in, thus making her feel passionately about her work, was the right decision. If she had stayed in the job where she wasn't genuinely enthusiastic about the work, she would not have achieved success for herself or the organization. She told me she now recognizes what makes her tick, but she also understands others are motivated differently. She described a colleague of hers at the diverse PR firm who was extremely good at his job and loved it. The difference is her colleague was thrilled by each new challenge to create publicity and garner media coverage, regardless of who or what was being publicized. Neither she nor her former colleague is wrong for the source of their inspiration; to the contrary, they are to be commended for understanding themselves and finding jobs that trigger their passion to perform.

If you are not passionate in your job, consider whether it's the work itself or the organization. When you can identify what makes you want to perform and what holds you back, you will be closer to finding a job that connects with your passion. Another consideration in the passion-for-work equation is talent. Once again drawing on the sports analogy, Mingledorff points out that you need to honestly assess your abilities when looking for a realistic match between passion and career.

> "I think that to be a rip roaring success you have to have ability. I don't think you can go further than your ability goes. I can have tremendous passion around tennis, but I don't have the ability of Jimmy Connors. I will never be as good as Jimmy Connors. Now Jimmy Connors could never be as good as he is if he didn't have passion around being a tennis player. To be world class takes both passion and ability."[58]

This statement echoes Covey's advice to find the "work that taps your talent and fuels your passion." It would be wonderful if all of the people who read this book are both passionate in their jobs and have associates who share that passion. Sadly, this will not be the case, as many people show up at work, punch in, and go through the motions with no enthusiasm or emotional commitment. As a leader, it is important for you to see signs and continually gauge the passion levels in your employees. Who is chronically late? Who never sacrifices a break, lunch, or vacation for work? Who is consistently punctual and willing to stay late? Who is excited by opportunities for advancement and personal growth?

The associates who demonstrate passion are potential stars, so ongoing development is your primary leadership responsibility to them. If a typically passionate associate begins to show signs of apathy and a lack of enthusiasm or commitment, a leader needs to notice this and investigate where the problem lies. The individuals who don't demonstrate passion will not serve themselves, you, or the organization to the best of their abilities. Perhaps they are misfits in the work assignments, or perhaps they don't fit in the organizational environment. Whatever the case, it is your responsibility to help ignite their passion. If you don't succeed, encourage them to explore the questions and considerations for finding that magical combination of passion and work. Perhaps there is a different position for them in your organization, or perhaps they need to look elsewhere.

Ensuring your employees "buy in" to the company with a passionate commitment is critical to everyone's success. According to Ronald Lazof, a leading management consultant, every employee in an organization needs to feel a "personal passion" for the business, because failing to have that will ultimately cause the business to fail. He writes:

> In short, if you have Personal Passion from every stakeholder in your business, cherish it, respect it and work hard to maintain and enhance its vigor. If you have Personal Passion from some of, but not all of, your stakeholders, learn from those with the Passion and enlist them in spreading your joint Personal Passion to everyone in the company. If you do not have Personal Passion for your business, or have it and can't communicate it or don't have an environment amendable to its continual and constant propagation—sell the business—quick—because your competitors will sense this weakness and maximize THEIR Personal Passion in the marketplace to your company's immediate and ruinous detriment.[59]

Passion Is Potential

Passion has been equated to purpose and power, and now potential. Only with passion will you have the unwavering conviction that what you are trying to achieve is possible. You have to passionately believe in the organization's mission and its products, services, and employees. Passion will give you the confidence to reach for your goals, no matter how ambitious or far-reaching. It unleashes your potential. An extraordinary achievement is always a possibility, but only the courage and conviction that come from passion will enable you to attain that satisfaction and success. If you are a passionate leader, the potential for greatness is within you and all of your associates.

Passion—Seek It for Yourself

When life is full of passion, it is colorful, exciting, exhilarating, and fulfilling. Without passion, life seems dull, boring, uninspiring, and lackluster. While individuals can't run full-steam on adrenaline at all times, there has to be enough passion present to counteract the times that require simple perseverance. You owe it to yourself to ensure you are actively pursuing what you are passionate about.

A young associate of mine once told me about a leader who had a lasting, positive impact on his life. The leader was his fifth grade teacher, a passionate educator who also launched an after-school chess club and coached several sports teams. From this teacher, the young man began to learn that challenging yourself physically and mentally was truly rewarding and that hard work and discipline would result in self-satisfaction. The most important lesson he learned, and one that still comes to his mind years later, is how that teacher responded when a student complained that something was "boring." Early in the school year the teacher had taught the students, upon hearing someone say "boring," to thump their hands rhythmically on their desks and chant in unison "boring people are easily bored." Hearing this over and over throughout the year, and having himself brought on the chant more than once, he gained the understanding that some tasks or activities are exciting while others seem more tedious, but your attitude and perspective are a personal choice.

Work and personal responsibilities are full of chores that can't be avoided whether we find them exciting or not. Therefore, it is in our best interests to engage in work and personal activities that coincide with our individual passions. When you have to get through your chores, it will be a lot easier if passion is present in the big picture. If you discover you are generally feeling lackluster and unenthused at work or in your personal life, remember that this is a choice. Why choose to be bored when you can choose to have a life full of energy and excitement? Assess what areas of your life seem to be fulfilling and in what respects you feel the passion missing. Determine what you want and what really excites you, then pursue it. Although it may require some soul searching, each and every one of us can identify something we care deeply about, something that really excites us, and something we really want to achieve. The things that spark your passion are actually the easiest to incorporate into your life because you will have the drive, determination, and faith to make them happen.

ASK THESE QUESTIONS TO CLARIFY YOUR SELF FOCUS

- Do you know anybody who has been passed over for a promotion? What happened to that person? Have you ever been passed over for a promotion you wanted? Why did that happen?

- Sometimes we never find out about an opportunity for promotion within our organization. If you answered "no" to the question above, how do you know you did not lose a promotion without even knowing you were being considered?

- If you have been in your current job for five years or more, is there anything you should be doing to prepare for your next job? Has the organization given you any hints about what you should do?

- If you have been in your job for less than a couple of years, does the company have a plan for you? Does it fit your expectations? If it does, are you ready to move to the next job? If not, what do you need to do to get ready?

- Have you done a SWOT analysis on yourself? If not, prepare the analysis and then ask yourself what you have learned. Show the analysis to somebody whose judgment you trust and ask that person to evaluate it.

- What is your long-term goal? Where do you want your life to be in ten years? In twenty years? Is there a match between your life goals and the career track you are on? If there is a divergence, what can you do to bring these two together?

- What are you going to do tomorrow to help you achieve your goals for the next year? What about next week? Develop a list of at least ten action plans for next week.

Only when you as an individual consistently nurture yourself will you be able to fully and selflessly give your best to your associates. This is particularly true in regards to passion. If you lack the passion to lead, lack passion for your job, or fail to incorporate passion into your life, you will not reach your full potential as a leader or individual. If you make the promise to yourself to always seek and embrace passion as an essential aspect of your life and to apply all of the leadership principles to yourself, success and personal fulfillment are yours for the taking.

Case Study

Charlie and Jane lived in Chicago and had been married for two years. They were both passionate about their careers, and that passion had translated to success and promotions. Jane was the executive chef of a small restaurant that had gained local acclaim for creative gourmet cuisine. She had begun to receive personal recognition after a journalist from a national gourmet magazine visited the restaurant and wrote a complimentary review. Her goals to run the kitchen at a big-name restaurant and ultimately open her own were proceeding according to her plan.

Charlie started his career as a sales representative for a textile company. He really enjoyed his work and was extremely loyal to his company because the upper management had consistently treated him well and rewarded his successes. The year he and Jane got married, he exceeded his sales goals by 100 percent. In addition to financial bonuses, his company awarded him a week-long vacation in Jamaica that enabled him to treat his wife to a wonderful honeymoon. Following that banner year, he was promoted to Midwest regional sales manager and continued to shine in his performance.

Five months ago, Charlie was invited to a meeting at the corporate headquarters and was given another opportunity for a promotion. He was asked to become the operations manager of the company's plant in a small town in South Carolina. The chance to advance his career to the next level was thrilling to Charlie, but the relocation and lifestyle changes were issues he would have to discuss with Jane. In addition to the consideration of how this would impact her career, he knew it would also be a challenge on a personal level. She had grown up in the Midwest and all of her family and friends lived close by.

The two debated the pros and cons of the move and within a month had made the firm decision for Charlie to accept the promotion. Jane was crushed that she would have to leave the job that she loved so much but was determined to make the best of it for her husband's benefit. She felt it would be unfair to hold him back in his career, and whereas he had a long history with his company, she could easily start over at a different restaurant. Furthermore, his income far exceeded hers, and they wanted to put money aside so they could start a family. Even if the pay was less for her, she was certain that she could find work at a local restaurant and eventually open her own.

Now living and working in South Carolina, Charlie is thriving. His leadership skills have enabled him to improve productivity at the plant, which has had a favorable impact on the company's revenue. He has developed a good rapport with his staff and has initiated new employee reward programs that boosted morale and made him a popular new face in the community. Jane is having the opposite experience. There are no gourmet restaurants in town, so the only job she could find was the head cook at a restaurant that is part of a national chain. She has no chance to use her own recipes or creativity, and the kitchen and wait staff appear to go through the motions with little regard to quality and service.

The fact that Jane is miserable and dreads going to work is obvious to Charlie, and he suggests she quit working at the restaurant. This sparks yet another argument; arguments have become increasingly common since their move. "Staying home alone all day while you're at work certainly won't make me happy, and honestly we need the second income," Jane says. While Charlie silently ponders this dilemma, Jane continues her lament. "Even if we could put practicality aside, I miss the gratification of using my talent to create wonderful meals. Not to mention the fun of working with people who are equally excited to please customers and provide a memorable dining experience."

Should Jane quit her job? If so, then what?

Whether for financial or personal reasons, it is unfortunately true that people sometimes end up in jobs for which they have no passion. When an individual finds himself or herself in this situation, it is time to start looking for a new job immediately. If you lack passion for your work, you will ultimately not perform well and not achieve success. If you don't quit yourself, it is likely you will be fired because your performance won't match the company's expectations. However difficult it may seem to overcome the obstacles and challenges that arise from finances or family obligations, you owe it to yourself to find a solution. Passion is not an optional part of the work equation; it is a must for success.

In Jane's case, she is so unhappy in her job it could destroy her emotional well-being and possibly her marriage. She needs to take a step back and make an honest assessment of why she is so unhappy. Is it just a result of the constraints imposed by cooking for a chain restaurant and the staff's apathy? Is she perhaps being unfair and viewing the staff harshly because they are small-town folk with different ways than metropolitan city workers? If she can truly assimilate into the town's lifestyle and community, then she should have many options for work and fulfilling her passion.

Since the town lacks a gourmet restaurant, she could explore the option of opening her own and also training her staff to work according to her standards and expectations. The food and format would likely be different than what is popular in Chicago, but designing a restaurant and menu that appeal to the locals would be a creative challenge for her. Another option would be to start a catering business for weddings and special events. She could also reinvent herself to some degree and consider starting a cooking school or compiling her recipes into a cookbook she could promote and sell online. She could open a restaurant consulting business and travel to various towns and cities in the area and help train the staff for professionalism and also give cooking instruction to the chef and kitchen staff. She might come up with her own product line of home-cooked specialty items and sell them at farmer's markets and town fairs. There are numerous options for her to pursue her passion, and she needs to start looking for the right situation now.

LEADERSHIP TIP

Ask yourself if these apply to you. If your answer to many of these is "no," then perhaps you need to consider whether there is a different job or organization in which you would be passionate.

- Do you gladly go to work early or stay late in order to excel?
- Do you frequently review your expectations and goals to make sure you are on track to meet them—and then beat them?
- Are you motivated more by the pleasure of your work than by the amount of your paycheck?
- Do you seek out ways to create enthusiasm and drive in your coworkers?
- Would your coworkers describe you as dedicated to the organization and its bottom line?
- Do you truly believe in the organization's mission and goals?
- Do you love most aspects of your work?
- Are you optimistic that you can achieve the goals that are set for you, even if they are a big step above the status quo?
- Do you spend some of your free time doing things such as reading or networking in order to enhance or improve your job performance?
- Is this your dream job?

These questions are not easy and require you to be honest with yourself. If you are not passionate about your work, you are lacking a key ingredient for success. Since success is the reward for hard work, it makes sense to find a job that brings out your passion.

EPILOGUE

Leadership Revisited—From Love to Passion

Our journey began with understanding the role of love in setting the tone of the relationship with your associates and concluded with a focus on creating a positive self-concept and being a leader to yourself. Between committing to honing your capacity to love associates and the role of loving and leading yourself, you must set expectations, make a correct assignment, focus on development, provide effective evaluation, deliver timely rewards, implement systems, embrace humor, honor integrity, and pursue passion. These leadership practices are necessary to foster, encourage, and assure peak performance from your associates. However, the real intensity of your efforts must be on yourself.

The role of leader places a burden on you that cannot be treated lightly. When you were an individual performer, your capacity to deliver results was the true measure of your success. As a leader, you will probably continue to do tasks that generate results for your organization, but your true measure of success shifts dramatically. You must help your associates achieve success as individuals and as a team. You must not allow the term *leader* to confuse you. You are not leading the work; you are leading the worker and other leaders.

BIBLIOGRAPHY

Chapter 1: Love—Friends Like but Leaders Love

Bennis, Warren and David A. Heenan. *Co-Leaders*. New York: John Wiley and Sons, 1999.

Bennis, Warren. *On Becoming a Leader*. Reading: Addison-Wesley, 1989.

Collins, James C. and Jerry I. Porras. *Built to Last*. New York: Harper Business, 1994.

DePree, Max. *Leadership Is an Art*. New York: Doubleday, 1989.

Gardner, John W. *On Leadership*. New York: The Free Press, 1990.

Gellerman, Saul W. *Management by Motivation*. New York: American Management Association, 1968.

Kotter, John P. *The Leadership Factor*. New York: The Free Press, 1988.

Kotter, John P. *What Leaders Really Do*. Boston: Harvard Business Review Book, 1999.

Levinson, Harry. *The Exceptional Executive: A Psychological Conception*. Cambridge: Harvard University Press, 1968.

Levinson, Harry. *The Great Jackass Fallacy*. Boston: Division of Research Graduate School of Business Administration Harvard University, 1973.

Maxwell, John C. *The Twenty-One Irrefutable Laws of Leadership: Follow Them and People Will Follow You*. Nashville: Thomas Nelson, 1998.

McGregor, Douglas. *The Human Side of Enterprise*. New York: McGraw-Hill, 1960.

Ouchi, William G. *Theory Z*. New York: Avon Publishers, 1981.

Potter, Beverly A. *Changing Performance on the Job*. New York: American Management Associations Publications Group, 1980.

Chapter 2: Expectations—Setting the Bar Sets the Tone

Allen, Louis A. *Making Managerial Planning More Effective.* New York: McGraw-Hill, 1982.

Augustine, Norman R. *Augustine's Laws.* New York: Viking Penguin, 1968.

Crosby, Philip B. *Quality Is Free.* New York: McGraw-Hill, 1979.

Drucker, Peter R. *Management: Tasks, Responsibilities and Practices.* New York: Harper and Row, 1973.

Goldratt, Eliyahu M. *The Goal.* Croton-on-the Hudson: North River Press, 1992.

Grove, Andrew S. *High Output Management.* New York: Random House, 1983.

Machiavelli, Niccolo. *The Prince.* New York: The New American Library of World Literature, 1952.

Tichy, Noel M. and Sherman Stratford. *Control Your Destiny or Someone Else Will.* New York: Currency Doubleday, 1993.

Chapter 3: Assignment—Square Pegs in Round Holes Never Fit!

Buckingham, Marcus and Curtis Coffman. *First, Break All the Rules.* New York: Simon and Schuster, 1999.

Champy, James. *Reengineering Management.* New York: Harper Collins, 1995.

Collins, James C. *Good to Great: Why Some Companies Make the Leap…and Others Don't.* New York: Harper Collins, 2002.

Fear, Richard A. *The Evaluation Interview.* New York: McGraw-Hill, 1978.

Jick, Todd D., Rosabeth Moss Kanter, and Barry A. Stein. *The Challenge of Organizational Change.* New York: The Free Press, 1992.

Lorsch, Jay W. and Thomas J. Tierney. *Aligning the Stars.* Boston: Harvard Business School Press, 2002.

Mintzberg, Henry. *The Structuring of Organizations.* Englewood Cliffs: Prentice Hall, 1979.

Chapter 4: Development—The Good Get Better, the Best Excel!

Byham, William C., PhD. *Zapp! The Lightning of Empowerment.* New York: Harmony Books, 1988.

Connellan, Thomas K. *How to Improve Human Performance.* New York: Harper and Row, 1978.

Drucker, Peter F. *The Frontiers of Management.* New York: Truman Talley Books, 1986.

Gordon, Thomas, Dr. *Leader Effectiveness Training*. Solana Beach: Wyden Books, 1977.

Harry, Mikel and Richard Schroeder. *Six Sigma*. New York: Doubleday, 2000.

Imai, Masaaki. *Kaizen*. New York: Random House Business Division, 1986.

Johnson, Harold E. *Mentoring for Exceptional Performance*. Glendale: Griffin Publishing Group, 1997.

Kotter, John P. *Leading Change*. Boston: Harvard Business School Press, 1996.

Senge, Peter M. *The Fifth Discipline: The Art and Practice of the Learning Organization*. New York: Doubleday, 1990.

Chapter 5: Evaluation—Leaders Succeed by Making Judgments

Batten, Joe D. *Tough-Minded Leadership*. New York: AMACOM, 1989.

Conner, Daryl R. *Managing at the Speed of Change*. New York: Villard Books, 1993.

Covey, Stephen R. *Principle-Centered Leadership*. New York: Simon and Schuster, 1992

———. *The 7 Habits of Highly Effective People*. New York: Simon and Schuster, 1989.

McConkey, Dale D. *How to Manage by Results*. New York: AMACOM, 1983.

Ogawa, Morimasa. *Pana Management*. Tokyo: PHP Institute, 1991.

Peters, Thomas J. and Robert H. Waterman. *In Search of Excellence: Lessons from America's Best Run Companies*. New York: Harper and Row, 1981.

Shorris, Earl. *The Oppressed Middle: Politics of Middle Management*. Garden City: Anchor Press/Doubleday, 1981.

Wheatley, Margaret J. *Leadership and the New Science*. San Francisco: Berrett-Koehler Publishers, 1992.

Chapter 6: Rewards—An Organization Elicits the Behavior It Rewards

Augustine, Norman R. *Augustine's Laws*. New York: Viking Penguin, 1968.

Chapter 7: Systems—Structure Frees the Mind to Be Creative

Fox, Justin. *"What Ben Franklin Can Teach Execs"*, *Fortune*. March, 2006.

Chapter 8: Humor – Lead with Humble Humor not Hubris

Kiffer, Jerome, MA. *Department of Health Psychology and Applied Psychotherapy*. Cleveland: The Cleveland Clinic Fornation, 2002.

Chapter 9: Integrity – Begin Every Action with a Commitment to Integrity

Granirer, David. *"Using Humor at Work"*. Retreived from www.granirer.com/ ART-0005.htm.

Melone, Linda. *"Laughing All the Way to the Bank"*. OC Metro: July 20, 2006.

Paulson, Terry L. *Making Humor Work*. Boston: Course Technology, 1989.

Shepell, Warren. *"Lighten Up: Humor in the Workplace"*. Retreived from www.warrenshepell.com/articles /humor/asp.

Van Oech, Roger. *A Whack on the Side of the Head*. New York: Time Warner Books Group, 1998.

Paulson, Terry L. *Making Humor Work*. Boston: Course Technology, 1989.

Weinstein, Matt. *Managing to Have Fun*. New York: A Fireside Book, 1996.

Chapter 10: Passion Drives Purpose and Performance

National Business Ethics Survey 2005. Washington DC: Ethics Resource Center, 2005.

Epilogue: Leadership Revisited: From Love to Passion

Bossidy, Larry and Ram Charan. *Execution*. New York: Crown Business, 2002.

Clavell, James. *The Art of War by Sun Tzu*. New York: Delacorte Press, 1983.

Cox, Allan. *The Making of the Achiever*. New York: Dodd, Meade, 1984.

Drucker, Peter F. *Managing in Turbulent Times*. New York: Harper and Row Publishers, 1980.

Gardner, John W. *Self-Renewal*. New York: W.W. Norton, 1995.

Heenan, David A. *Double Lives: Crafting Your Life of Work and Passion for Untold Success*. Palo Alto: Davies-Black, 2002.

Johnson, Spencer, MD. *Who Moved My Cheese?*. New York: G.P. Putnam's Sons, 1998.

Kanter, Rosabeth Moss. *The Change Masters*. New York: Simon and Schuster, 1983.

O'Toole, James. *Vanguard Management*. Garden City, NY: Doubleday, 1985.

Peters, Tom. *Thriving on Chaos*. New York: Alfred A. Knopf, 1987.

Waterman, Robert H., Jr. *The Renewal Factor*. Toronto: Bantam Books, 1987.

ENDNOTES

1   John William Gardner, *On Leadership* (New York: The Free Press, Inc. Pgs. 1990), 3–4.

2   John P. Kotter, *On What Leaders Really Do* (Boston: Harvard Business Review Book, 1999), 16.

3   Joe D. Batten, *Tough-Minded Leadership* (New York: American Management Association, 1989), 2.

4   Gardner, *On Leadership*, 1.

5   James C. Collins and Jerry I. Porras, *Built to Last: Successful Habits of Visionary Companies* (New York: Harper Collins, 1994), 213.

6   John P. Kotter, *The Leadership Factor* (New York: The Free Press, 1988), 124.

7   Saul W. Gellerman, *Management by Motivation* (New York: American Management Association, 1968), 23.

8   Morimasa Ogawa, *Pana Management* (Tokyo: PHP Institute, 1990), 47.

9   David A. Heenan, *Double Lives: Crafting Your Life of Work and Passion for Untold Success* (Palo Alto: Davies-Black, 2002), 222.

10   John C. Maxwell, *The Twenty-One Irrefutable Laws of Leadership: Follow Them and People Will Follow You* (Nashville: Thomas Nelson, 1998), 101.

11   Allan J. Cox, *The Making of the Achiever* (New York: Dodd, Meade, 1985), 12.

12   Warren G. Bennis, *On Becoming a Leader* (Reading: Addison-Wesley, 1989), 163.

13 Beverly A. Potter, *Changing Performance on the Job* (New York: American Management Associations Publications Group, 1980), 67.

14 John W. Gardner, *The Individual and the Innovative Society* (New York: W.W. Norton, 1995), 10.

15 Thomas Gordon, *Leader Effectiveness Training* (Solana Beach: Wyden Books, 1977), 20.

16 Norman R. Augustine, *Augustine's Laws* (New York: Viking Penguin, 1983, 1986), 363.

17 Batten, *Tough-Minded Leadership*, 142.

18 Niccolo Machiavelli, *The Prince* (New York: The New American Library of World Literature, 1952), 49.

19 John P. Kotter, *Leading Change* (Boston: Harvard Business School Press, 1996), 185.

20 James C. Collins, *Good to Great: Why Some Companies Make the Leap… and Others Don't* (New York: Harper Collins, 2001), 41.

21 Henry Mintzberg, *The Structuring of Organizations* (Englewood Cliffs: Prentice Hall, 1979), 83.

22 Richard A. Fear, *The Evaluation Interview* (New York: McGraw-Hill, 1978), 12.

23 Collins, *Good to Great*, 126.

24 Andrew S. Grove, *High Output Management* (New York: Random House, 1983), 203.

25 Jay W. Lorsch and Thomas J. Tierney, *Aligning the Stars* (Boston: Harvard Business School Press, 2002), 2.

26 Spencer Johnson, *Who Moved My Cheese? An Amazing Way to Deal with Change in Your Work and Your Life* (New York: G.P. Putman's Sons, 1998), 60.

27 Stephen R. Covey, *Principle-Centered Leadership* (New York: Simon and Schuster, 1992), 246.

28 Harry Levinson, *The Exceptional Executive: A Psychological Conception* (London: Oxford University Press, 1968, 1970), 133.

29 Gordon, *Leader Effectiveness Training*, 8.

30 Masaaki Imai, *Kaizen* (New York: McGraw-Hill, 1986), 3.

31 Kenneth Blanchard, Patricia Zigarmi, and Drea Zigarmi, *Leadership and the One Minute Manager* (New York: Blanchard Management Corporation, 1985), 53.

32 Marcus Buckingham and Curtis Coffman, *First, Break All the Rules: What the World's Greatest Managers Do Differently* (New York: Simon and Schuster, 1999), 57.

33 Douglas McGregor, *The Human Side of Enterprise* (New York: McGraw-Hill, 1978), 87.

34 Grove, *High Output Management*, 188.

35 Augustine, *Augustine's Laws*, 364.

36 Justin Fox, "What Ben Franklin Can Teach Execs," *Fortune* (March 9, 2006). Retrieved from http://money.cnn.com/2006/03/08/magazines/fortune/pluggedin_fortune/index.htm.

37 Jerome F. Kiffer, MA, Department of Health Psychology and Applied Psychophysiology, The Cleveland Clinic Foundation, 2002.

38 Linda Melone, "Laughing All the Way to the Bank," *OCMetro* (July 20, 2006).

39 Ibid.

40 Ron Culberson, FUNsulting.

41 Melone, "Laughing All the Way to the Bank."

42 Matt Weinstein, *Managing to Have Fun* (New York: A Fireside Book, 1996).

43 Warren Shepell, "Lighten Up: Humour in the Workplace." Retrieved from www.warrenshepell.com/articles/humour.asp.

44 David Granirer, "Using Humor at Work." Retrieved from www.granirer.com/ART-0005.htm.

45 Matt Weinstein, *Managing to Have Fun*.

46 Roger van Oech, *A Whack on the Side of the Head* (New York: Time Warner Book Group, 1998).

47 Terry L. Paulson, PhD, *Making Humor Work* (Boston: Course Technology, 1989).

48 "AmEx's Ken Chenault Talks about Leadership, Integrity and the Credit Card Business," *Knowledge@Wharton* (April 20, 2005).

49 Ibid.

50 *National Business Ethics Survey 2005* (Washington DC: Ethics Resource Center, October 14, 2005).

51 "Winners Never Cheat: Lessons for Today's Business Leaders," *Knowledge@Wharton* (June 01, 2005).

52 Ibid.

53 Ibid.

54 Jonathan Byrnes, "The Essence of Leadership." Retrieved from http://hbswk.hbs.edu/archive/4983.html.

55 Stephen R. Covey, *The 8th Habit: From Effectiveness to Greatness* (New York: Free Press, 2004).

56 Michele Payn-Knoper, "The Light of Leadership." Retrieved from http://www.michelepaynknoper.com/articles/passionleaderleaderleadership.html.

57 Marie J. Kane, "CEOs Speak on Leadership: Vision and Passion." Retrieved from http://www.refresher.com/!mjkvision.html.

58 Ibid.

59 Ronald C. Lazof, "Personal Passion: The Art of Business." Retrieved from http://www.refresher.com/!rclpassion.html.

BUY A SHARE OF THE FUTURE IN YOUR COMMUNITY

These certificates make great holiday, graduation and birthday gifts that can be personalized with the recipient's name. The cost of one S.H.A.R.E. or one square foot is $54.17. The personalized certificate is suitable for framing and will state the number of shares purchased and the amount of each share, as well as the recipient's name. The home that you participate in "building" will last for many years and will continue to grow in value.

THIS CERTIFIES THAT

YOUR NAME HERE

HAS INVESTED IN A HOME FOR A DESERVING FAMILY

1985-2005

TWENTY YEARS OF BUILDING FUTURES IN OUR
COMMUNITY ONE HOME AT A TIME

1200 SQUARE FOOT HOUSE @ $65,000 = $54.17 PER SQUARE FOOT
This certificate represents a tax deductible donation. It has no cash value.

Here is a sample SHARE certificate:

YES, I WOULD LIKE TO HELP!

I support the work that Habitat for Humanity does and I want to be part of the excitement! As a donor, I will receive periodic updates on your construction activities but, more importantly, I know my gift will help a family in our community realize the dream of homeownership. **I would like to SHARE in your efforts against substandard housing in my community!** *(Please print below)*

PLEASE SEND ME _____ SHARES at $54.17 EACH = $ $_____

In Honor Of: _____

Occasion: (Circle One)   *HOLIDAY*   *BIRTHDAY*   *ANNIVERSARY*

     OTHER: _____

Address of Recipient: _____

Gift From: _____ *Donor Address:* _____

Donor Email: _____

I AM ENCLOSING A CHECK FOR $ $_____ PAYABLE TO HABITAT FOR HUMANITY <u>OR</u> PLEASE CHARGE MY VISA OR MASTERCARD *(CIRCLE ONE)*

Card Number _____ Expiration Date: _____

Name as it appears on Credit Card _____ Charge Amount $ _____

Signature _____

Billing Address _____

Telephone # Day _____ Eve _____

PLEASE NOTE: Your contribution is tax-deductible to the fullest extent allowed by law.
Habitat for Humanity • P.O. Box 1443 • Newport News, VA 23601 • 757-596-5553
www.HelpHabitatforHumanity.org

Breinigsville, PA USA
25 February 2010
233224BV00001B/1/P